Praise for *Focused and On Fire*

"If you've ever fired yourself up, or envisioned scoring a game-winning goal, you're drawing upon the power of your mind. Through my work with Lisa, I started out lost and lacking confidence, but she helped me find a mental routine and the head space to dial into my game like I'd never done before. As a former nationally ranked athlete and later coach at Stanford, Lisa Mitzel understands how to excel and enjoy competing at any level. Mapping precise thoughts and actions will get you to your goal. After training with Lisa, I returned to soccer with a new poise and set of skills. I took on new challenges for my team and in many other endeavors as well. Lisa's stories and curriculum are not just about sport—this book will incite patience, personal knowledge, and teach you how to achieve in life." —**Gabriella Kaplan, former U.S. Girls National Team and Member Women's Soccer Team, Harvard University**

"As a coach of 11 Olympians throughout the past 50 years, I truly understand the absolute necessity of having mental training as an integral component at all levels of competitive gymnastics. Lisa Mitzel was one of my gymnasts and as such, demonstrated the ability to persevere, overcome adversity and to relish the challenges of elite level sports. A coach needs to address the physical aspects of the training process, but it takes a specialist in mental training to take the athlete to the ultimate level. Lisa has produced her book, *Focused and On Fire* to accomplish this. Her experiences as an athlete and her education as a mental training expert will give coaches and athletes the ability to not only believe in their goals but to embrace the challenges of those goals and reach the reality in the process." —**Mary Wright, Olympic Games, Coach for New Zealand, Coach of 11 Olympians representing NZ, Canada and the USA**

"My greatest hope for my children is to do well and have success, but that holds little value if they're experiencing anxiety and stress. My daughter, Katherine, had been training with excellent gymnastics coaches and advancing, but suddenly she faced huge fears, seemingly out of no where, especially on beam. She froze up, mentally and physically, and lost all confidence. Her coaches were perplexed and tried to help her through it but nothing was working. My husband and I wondered if she should quit due to the frustration and stress she was feeling. Then we heard about Lisa and her expertise in mental training, so we decided to give it a try. I'm so glad we did! Katherine trained and learned new mindsets and ways to get calm and focused. She enjoyed her sessions with Lisa, creating personal scripts, doing exercises, drawing pictures and making signs—it was fun. My daughter has grown a new level of poise and tenacity, she's moved up, and her coaches are delighted. *Focused and On Fire* is Lisa's masterful program, a friendly and wise book that is so important for parents to share with their young athletes." —**Sarah Clayton, mother to a happy and tenacious 12 yr old gymnast**

"Rising through the ranks of high school sports in northern California can be treacherous—the landscape of athletes, parents and even coaches is littered with doubters and haters along the way. My son, Andrew (16, baseball), had aspirations to play at the highest level possible in his sport. I met Lisa through a good friend and have always been a believer in using strong mental skills to rise toward the highest potential. Although the "book" on my son's baseball career is in its earliest chapters, the mental training he has completed and the results from this focus with Lisa Mitzel has been profound—my son has grown to develop a tremendous sense of inner confidence, as well as an ability to block out the negativity he comes across in dugouts, classrooms or passing by in high school hallways; focusing on his game and his performance without nervousness or doubt. My favorite moment was watching him at a Division I camp for a Top 5 national program, playing at an elite level that simply wouldn't have been possible, mentally, without the work developed by Lisa and trained rigorously by my son." —**James Bergeron, Managing Partner @ 108 Partners, Chairman, SportsPay, Menlo Park, CA**

"In running cross-country, the distance is hard and the pain is going to hit you… I dreaded that. I was distracted by doubts, fears, and often injuries. I didn't know what to focus on to keep me strong and confident. When I talked to Lisa, she seemed to know exactly my negative thoughts and started to coach me in mental training. I learned how to talk to myself with positive messages, and visualize myself running and getting through the pain to the finish line. I really improved, and I think any athlete will benefit from reading Lisa's book, *Focused and On Fire*. She definitely helped me!" —**Cross country and Track runner, Dartmouth College, High School Record Holder 800M, 1600M and 4x400**

"My teenage daughter faced debilitating fears in gymnastics, breaking down, and considered quitting. Her coaches did not know how to handle the situation. Fortunately, after meeting with Lisa and training with her mental skills curriculum, my daughter made improvements, built confidence, and enjoyed a successful level 10 gymnastics season. We believe Lisa's mental training program and philosophies are a wonderful gift for any athlete facing challenges and hoping to achieve their goals. My daughter is now looking forward to competing at the college level." —**Mother of Level 10 gymnast, Airborne Gymnastics**

"My golf game is a big part of my life. In order to get to the next level, I knew I needed to focus on my mental game. I contacted Lisa because of her success as an athlete and coach, and I knew she could help me win. We focused on multiple mental techniques to get me prepared for my tournaments. After working with Lisa for a year and a half, I won 2 amateur golf tournaments, was a semifinalist in the San Francisco City Championship and accomplished my long time goal of qualifying for a USGA Championship in 2016. I don't know if I would be where I am in my golf career, as well as my life, if I hadn't contacted Lisa." —**Ben Peters, Nationally-ranked amateur golfer**

"I've coached youth sports for many years, and often my daughter and her teams in basketball. When she became a serious high school track and cross-country runner, I saw her go from one of the best freshman in the school's history to struggling with injuries and doubt. Then we sought out Lisa Mitzel. Lisa is fantastic and she had strategies. Her expertise lies in both areas of the physical demands and the psychological training needed to be successful. My daughter learned and practiced the mental skills, her confidence grew, and she reached her goals. Mental training is key for any student-athlete who wants to succeed, and Lisa's book speaks to young athletes so they can not only understand, but truly feel inspired." —**Father, Youth Sports Coach, MBA, UCLA**

FOCUSED AND ON FIRE
The Athlete's Guide to
Mental Training & Kicking Butt

BY LISA MITZEL
NCAA National Champion, 6-Time All-American,
Member of 4 NCAA National Championship Teams

ISBN-13: 978-1548124410
ISBN-10: 1548124419

Little Mitz Publishing
First edition, June 2017

REACH • SWEAT • BELIEVE

LisaMitzel.com

Book designed by Judi Eichler Design Studio
JudiEichlerDesigns.com

For my mom, Lorie, and my sisters, Sheila and Julie. You are the first women role models in my life. You are amazing love, unending support, and the strong voices that shaped me.

In memory of Betty Mitzel, my grandmother, my enthusiastic cheerleader, and saver of Bingo money.

Table of Contents

Message from Lisa

As an athlete, all I wanted was to be 'good,' to keep rising to the top. And I did. I trained 25-30 hours a week as a gymnast, and I competed with the best, with Olympians; I was up there in that circle. I was fortunate to get a college scholarship to the University of Utah. Utah had won back-to-back national championships the two years before I arrived, and they wanted to keep on winning. Our coach was strict, practices were hard, and the women on the team were tough, which made me both nervous and motivated. But by the end of my four years at Utah, even with many injuries and surgeries, including a broken back, I was a national champion, a 6-time All-American, and our team won NCAA Nationals all four years in a row. It was truly unbelievable. We even met President Reagan in the White House.

MY, AREN'T YOU A PRETTY ONE.

PRESIDENT REAGAN   ME

But throughout my journey, I was critical of myself. I struggled in making mistakes in practice, and I wanted to be perfect. You know, the 'perfect 10.' It was a curse, but it drove me to work harder all the time. I was also an odd size. I am very tall—King Kong for a gymnast—a skyscraper. My legs are bowed. And my arms, gangly, skinny, and not very strong. I battled with criticizing myself, but I was lucky. Through positive messages and people, I learned to balance it all out.

LISA

MITZEL FAMILY

Growing up, my parents surrounded me with wise, kind advice: they told me we can work through any problem, and they filled me with the belief that good things are always coming—you just have to look for them. In practice and competition, I'd get nervous, jittery, painful butterflies, run to the bathroom and have diarrhea…blahh…but then it left me. Then I could zero in on my task, get laser-focused and do well. I was a serious kid, but also a happy kid. Instead of worrying about failing, I had faith and I prayed. I prayed a lot. I'm one of seven kids, and we went to church. In many rooms in our house, Jesus

YOU ARE LOVED

signs and messages said, I am loved, be curious, and know that God is always with me. I believed those messages with all my heart.

But to be honest, I don't think it's a God-thing as much as a *self-belief practice*. It's developing your own personal principles, and balancing criticism with being optimistic. I think athletes self-criticize because we want to be better. But that's one-sided and negative. So I envisioned what I wanted. I imagined accomplishing great things, and I saw myself performing like a champion. Positive energy draws in good fortune and good people. A mindset of hope and desire elicits grace in our path to reach higher. Especially when things seem unlikely. During a dark struggle, call on your inner drive and it will rally a light. Rally yourself! Be a light! And you will overcome.

I hope you love this book. I have coached and worked with many athletes over the years, and I always seem to relate to them since I experienced all the difficulties—sprains, fractures, surgeries, doubt, nervousness, and terrible fear, all so badly. So badly I cried for months and nearly quit. But I rose above it all and I transformed through the struggles. I also learned that in coaching, it's my positive energy and beliefs that connect to and spark my athletes to do well. It comes down to believing in yourself. And I was blessed to train with the best coaches, athletes, and sport psychologists in the country, who modeled and taught me how to use the tools to prepare my mind for success.

It's kind of funny…it still seems like a dream how lucky I've been.

But I think it's because, *I believed.*

Introduction

Who is the most important person in the entire world you will communicate with for the rest of your life? It's you. Yourself. Yet how much do you listen to others and think about what they say? And how much do you talk to others online, or on your phone, and care more about what they think of you?

If you want to master your mind in sports, or any area of life, you might consider talking and listening to yourself much more. Create your own world. Visit your own mind, your feelings, and you will be in tune.

All athletes, boys and girls in every sport, experience distraction. If you're an athlete, you'll get nervous at times and doubt your abilities. When people are watching, when the other team is tough, if you're worried about an injury or you don't want to lose, how do you keep your mind on the task at hand and feel confident? The simplest answer—it starts with a breath… Just breathing…And learning how to manage thoughts and feelings. Because you can. You really can.

If you play sports and want to do well, or if you're a parent or coach wanting to help your athlete, I suspect you have this book because you're curious. For athletes, I'm delighted you're interested! Because training your mind is a life-enhancing journey. It truly gives you personal power to succeed with the ability to feel clear and sure and more in control of your path.

This book is a result of over 30 years of training, competing, and coaching. My success is directly connected to my own time studying and working with sport psychologists, and then teaching the mental skills to my teams and athletes. I've developed a curriculum and I'm honored to share my experiences, beliefs, and stories with you. I coach athletes in mental skills from ages eight to thirty-eight. You can read the chapters in a row, or pick one at a time in any order you like. Parents or coaches can sit with younger athletes and talk about the tools, look at the pictures, practice breathing and relaxing, together. Take it one small step at a time, no matter what age. Slowing down is key to managing the mind. And you can make it fun and interesting.

The illustrations in this book are meant to be playful and smart. The girl often has an M on her clothing; her name is "Little Mitz." And the boy often has a J for "Jake." Most of the illustrations have a helpful message to emphasize the mental skills and positive mindsets in this book.

Whatever you want to do—overcome anxiety, focus better, gain more confidence, or accomplish a big goal—I know these mental skills can help you.

Chapter 1
Your Brain is a Muscle

Okay, your brain is not actually a muscle, but it's similar to a muscle. And in sports, athletes' bodies do amazing things, and so can your brain! But the thing is you need to train it.

Both the brain and body are information systems that keep learning and growing as you use them. With exercise, muscles get stronger, right? And inside the brain, it forms new connections. The key is to strengthen your body and stimulate your brain in a variety of ways so you can be your best.

As an athlete, you work hard. You train many repetitions to play your best. But what happens when you get nervous? Or distracted? Or you feel scared you're going to forget something, fall, or let someone down? Or…you look at your talented opponents and think: *What am I doing here? I'm not good enough.*

These are thoughts. Untrained thoughts can mess up all that hard work and preparation you did. Because, like your body, thoughts are powerful, and they need discipline.

Coaches teach sports technique, physical conditioning, and competition strategies. But for most athletes, that's not enough to consistently perform under pressure. You try to concentrate on your moves, but you second guess yourself or make mistakes. The mental stuff affects you. Your mind is not in control and it causes problems.

The key is to practice mentally. Recite positive messages to yourself to access them in a challenging moment. Relive your best plays to feel more confident. Review 3-5 moves every night at home in bed. Imagine everything in your mind, clearly. Live through intention.

When you take charge of your progress, you prepare your mind to be in full command.

Map it. Believe it. Achieve it.

We had nine women on the team for the '95-'96 season: three freshmen, four sophomores, one junior and one senior. Very small and very young. It was my first year as head coach at Stanford University for Women's Gymnastics. In the history of the program, they had made it once to the NCAA National Championships, and that was four years earlier. They wanted to break into that level again, yet talent was an issue. And worse than that, when they arrived for pre-season training I observed these young women, and they did not think or act like a top team. They lacked the confidence, drive, and 'grit.' I wanted to change that.

As a college gymnast in the 80s, I competed for the University of Utah. We were the best in the nation. During my four years on the team, we won four consecutive NCAA National Championships. It's true. Under Greg Marsden, one of the winningest coaches in college sports, I learned. We had extremely disciplined practices, killer conditioning, and consistent mental training with sport psychologist, Dr. Keith Henschen. The mental training was powerful, and, on top of that, Utah had fiercely determined athletes. Every gymnast trained with a boldness I admired. I was motivated every day by my teammates. They had 'sass' and vision. Greg drilled us into the strongest and leanest bodies, told us we would be the fittest team on the floor, and developed us into focused minds and exact performances. We would win...And we did.

I wanted to infuse *that* into Stanford.

In Fall pre-season training one day, I entered the Stanford gym with a map. We had talked with the team about their goal to make it to nationals and I had an idea. I unfolded the chart of The United States of America and showed it to the girls, saying, "Here we are in California." I tapped on Palo Alto. "Nationals are in..." and I pointed way across the map, "Tuscaloosa, Alabama."

I folded my arms and said: "We are going to Alabama."

Their eyes grew wide...and they smiled.

I had a red marker and made a red dot where we were in Palo Alto, and another red dot where we were going: Tuscaloosa. I taped the map to the wall in the gym, right by the bars.

"Every extra hard practice you do, we will draw a small red line toward Alabama. Every conditioning round. Every bike circuit. Every early morning aerobics. You will be stronger, more focused, and more disciplined than ever before. You will *become* a top team and you will *earn* your way to Alabama."

I could feel my own determination buzzing in my body, and as the team looked at me and the map, I could also feel their energy—it was palpable.

Over the following weeks, we drilled and drilled: lots of basics, solid technique, perfect form, repetition, repetition. We broke down the gymnasts physically till they cramped and moaned. It was exhausting…and thrilling. Then we had team talks. Intense talks. They were asked to reveal personal challenges, doubts, and fears—to acknowledge their own conflicts and struggles. The girls got to know each other deeply, and in kind, supported each other in every way. They pushed each other to overcome, to work harder, draw red lines on the map, and keep going and going… The drive began.

In the locker room, they kept a team journal. The women randomly took turns entering positive, inspiring messages to each other. Writing and reading those messages kept them hooked into believing Nationals was possible.

In the winter, we started competition. I said, "Now, you need to tell someone ten times a day—we're going to Nationals. A friend, parent, dog, anyone. Tell them you're going."

They paused, got quiet.

"This isn't bragging or wishing," I explained. "You are being assertive. You are taking action and spreading positive belief. You are saying what you want and what you will do."

They looked at each other, hesitant, but a new challenge stirred inside them.

Soon, I had daily phone messages, "Hey, Coach, we're going to Nationals! Coach, see you in Alabama. Coach, did you know we're going to Nationals? Hahaha."

They took it seriously; it was fun, and they started to become fierce. They strutted into the gym, arms swinging, and heads held higher. They shared with each other who they were telling, who was excited for them, and also, who believed in them. They kept marking red lines on the map. They were building mental powers. They were beginning to believe.

The season progressed; we competed every week. Going against UCLA, Arizona State, and other dynamic teams was not easy; we were not winning. We had to remind our Stanford gymnasts the journey is a process: "Keep your eyes on each other, focus on your performances. Don't watch the other team." They listened. They re-focused. And soon, our team was breaking Stanford school records. Other coaches and teams took notice, and our routines were getting solid scores from the judges. This was evidence. We were emerging as confident competitors.

In practice, we sat in a circle and imagined. We talked about Alabama, what Tuscaloosa looked like, the two-hour time difference, southern culture, which famous barbecue restaurant we'd eat at, and we performed mock national competition in our gym. During which, the team pretended to go against other teams at Nationals. We imagined being there, and rehearsed the determination and focus for 'the stage.'

As we approached NCAA Regionals, the lo-ng red dotted line on the map, from California to Alabama, was complete. When the team saw it, in some way it cemented all of their hard work. They had earned it. And by the time we arrived at Regionals, the Stanford team had evolved.

They had created courage and honed a calm stance. And before competing beam in meets, they blocked out everyone else. It was a mental ritual I taught them. They gathered in a circle, held hands, closed eyes, and stood very still… breathing….as one. The crowd made noise, music played, and our opponent rumbled. But our team focused solely on themselves. Going inward and connecting with each other gave them inner power—it made them believe in their abilities and the strength of the team's energy. We were one of the most consistent beam teams in every meet we competed.

Finally, after six months of preparation, the night arrived. NCAA Regional Championships were hosted at UCLA. Our team knew it was the deciding meet. I could feel the tension. After warm-ups, the petite nine women were dressed and set in sweats and ponytails. It was time to march into the arena for competition. We all gathered in a circle, put our hands in, took a deep breath and looked at each other. They smiled. And one of the women shouted, "Okay, let's do this! One, two, three" then everyone yelled, "Go Stanford!" They were ready.

You may not believe it, but that night in competition, it wasn't about Nationals. It was about who they were; who they had become as athletes; how they matured as competitors; who they wanted to be for each other. And, ohhh, how Stanford did it. With Athena-like valor, the gymnasts transcended, flying high, nailing dismounts, and peaking at Regionals. When it was all over, when the scores were in and double checked, Stanford University had qualified to the 1996 NCAA National Championships. Stanford Gymnastics was going to Alabama!

At Nationals, we did very well. We finished 9th in the country, the highest Stanford ever finished. We were a Top-10 team! One of the best!

Since then, the Stanford Women's Gymnastics Team has competed in 15 NCAA National Championships and is one of the premier teams in the country. They may even win a National title some day! But I often recall that year, that journey to Tuscaloosa, and how amazing it was. Sometimes I shake my head and think to myself…Nooo wayy, I can't believe it!

Develop a Higher Mind

When you prepare your mind, when you're in charge of your thoughts and feelings, you are developing a high-minded brain. When the Stanford Women's Gymnastics team competed at NCAA Regionals, their minds were fluid and focused, calm and confident. They were ready to perform. They had programmed their minds to excel at the right time. And their bodies responded.

Like muscles in your body, your brain will get stronger with exercise, mental exercise. Because, as you train your mind with specific practices, like visualizing, scripting, positive self-talk, and recall, you can master your thoughts and conquer every challenging moment.

The messages you say to yourself, the thoughts that occupy your mind, they form patterns; therefore, you need to create strong, positive patterns of thought.

Mindsets for Success

To develop your higher mind, in this book you will learn the six mental skills; you'll receive advice, tools, exercises, *and* positive mindsets.

A mindset is like a personal philosophy that governs how you think and act; how you approach situations, how you respond, and how you will be the most self-assured person in training and competition.

A clear mindset pilots you in overcoming frustration and obstacles as they arise. For example, a teacher may have a philosophy of kindness, a coach may reward hard work, a parent may emphasize completing chores before you invite a friend over. What is important about personal philosophies is that they guide you to learn and grow, to be a good person and to become your best in whatever you pursue.

As you follow your intention to create a powerful mind and spirit for sports, use the mindsets in this book; read them, write them down, post them on your bedroom wall and practice using them. When you choose higher-mind thinking, you truly can prosper.

Mindset: Volition

Volition is the powerful will inside you that aims to rise up, take action, and perform well. It is an all-encompassing desire; a personal attitude that is developed through your vision of your future self. You imagine doing the hard work, and little by little, you witness your own growth and strength. You learn that you can make progress. You believe you can achieve!

Examples of the Volition Mindset are often found in inspiring books and movies—all kinds. For many of the teams I've coached, I've shown specific sports films that foster a deep motivation to practice with commitment, and to imagine and believe in the extraordinary. Fun team parties with a movie and popcorn can be very inspiring. You can even watch the same type of motivating film with your family.

A short list of sports movies I recommend: *Cool Runnings, Hoosiers, Rudy, The Rookie, Bend it Like Beckham, Gracie, Blue Crush,* and *A League of their Own.* Regarding books, here are various titles, and depending on your age and sport, you can consider: *In these Girls, Hope is a Muscle: The True Story of Hoop Dreams* and *One Very Special Team* by Madeline Blais, *Athletic Shorts* by Chris Crutcher, *Roughnecks* by Thomas Cochran, *Friday Night Lights: A Town, a Team, and a Dream* by H.G. Bissinger, *Babe Didrikson: The Greatest All-Sport Athlete of All Time* by Susan Cayleff, *Damage* by A.M Jenkins, *The Greatest: Muhammad Ali* by Walter Dean Myers, *Game Face: What Does a Female Athlete Look Like?* by Jane Gottesman, *The Runner* by Cynthia Voigt, *My Losing Season: A Memoir* by Pat Conroy. Please, go to your library or local bookstore to peruse and search for inspiring and true sports stories. The characters and stories you'll find have struggles, passion, and true volition.

What happens to Volition during a Tough Time? Do you Give up or Persevere?

It's normal in sports to go through tough times—difficult practices, painful injuries, or a losing season—and you want to stop, go home, or sometimes, quit. Don't do it, don't give up. Because you are stronger than you think you are. Get back in tune with why you are playing sports and get help from a supportive friend or family member. When you think about and make decisions from your deepest desires, your own volition will stir inside you. Connect your mind to what you truly want, because you can keep going! When you persevere, positive voices and people will come into your life to help you. No kidding. It's happened to me and my athletes many times. So if you're on the verge of giving up, you're clearly going through a very hard time. But what about staying open-minded to the unknown? Many athletes quit when they're down. It's easy to give up then. But I suggest being patient, keep at it, and look for help. If you use mental skills, you'll feel good that you persevered. You'll know it took courage….and that it's inside you.

How much Time?

Mental training can be practiced in small increments of time. After initially learning and understanding the tools, you can practice anywhere from 5 - 15 minutes a day and your performance will improve gradually as you stick to a regimen. With two to three months of practice, you'll notice changes, a sharper focus and a growing confidence. To master these skills, you need a mental skills coach at times, and continual practice and application. And it's worth it! Consider all the training for sports. It's said there are 3 types:

1. Physical practice: fitness, flexibility, strength, speed, endurance, balance, and agility.

2. Technical elements: proficiency and accuracy in your sport; exact body positions/action.

3. Mental training: awareness and focus on your breath, thoughts, and body to be calm and confident; mind control to manage distractions and execute precise movement and the highest level of performance.

Sports medicine and getting treatments are also key for an athlete's preparation. Taking care of your body is essential to performing, and though it's not 'training,' it takes time. A treatment can be icing a knee, getting a sports massage, or getting a wrist, ankle, or shoulder taped up. These types of self-care can add 20 minutes before and/or after practice and games, so consider that in your schedule.

Overall, mental training accounts for at least *twenty percent of your time* toward playing and competing in sports. But practicing the mental skills can account for *eighty percent of your success*. Because when your mind is filled with strong, focused thoughts, you are highly likely to perform well. You may not be able to rely on your coach to learn and practice the mental skills, and that's okay. Expand yourself by reading this book or online articles, talk to your parents or a teammate, step into curiosity, and begin to learn and practice the tools. You can, you can, you can master your mind for sports.

Kick-butt Practices and Exercises for Chapter 1

Exercise: What do you Want!

To get in tune with and create your volition mindset, you must know your desires. What you think and say are important, and then know what steps you'll take to get it. So, what do you want? Follow these instructions:

1. "I want a good grade on my test." If this is what you truly want, then how will you achieve it? It's important to study, right? Then say, "I will study to get a good grade."

2. "I want stronger abs." If this is what you truly want, then how will you achieve it? It's important to do crunches/ab exercises, yes? Then say, "I will do fifty crunches today."

Think of what you want. Create your own words of desire. Then say how you will achieve it.

This exercise is the way to acknowledge what you want, how you will achieve it, and that it all starts with your inner desire. These examples are small in comparison to winning a game or championship. Start small and practice using your volition. Write down at least one wish or desire. Read it, say it, and keep using it to encourage yourself. Take action with the volition mindset!

Exercise: Develop your Higher Mind and Make an Overall Plan

Life is a series of moments, choices, and actions. With a complete plan to grow and improve in sports, success will come. From the list provided, check off the items you are currently doing well. Circle the items you want to start doing or want to make improvements.

- 1. I EAT healthy foods and hydrate, daily.
- 2. I READ about successful teams & athletes.
- 3. I LEARN from experienced coaches and role models.
- 4. I WRITE down my goals, big and small, and check off the steps as I achieve them.

- 5. I SCHEDULE my weekly plan on a calendar and follow it.
- 6. I SLEEP plenty of hours at night, 8-9 hours on average, and I have energy!
- 7. I CARE for my body and do treatments before and after practice & games.

22

- **8** I TALK & LISTEN to positive friends, coaches, and wise people, and I feel supported.

- **9** I PRACTICE MENTAL SKILLS and POSITIVE MINDSETS to guide my thoughts and my performance.

Reviewing this list once a month can help keep you in touch with your volition of wanting to do well in sports. When you take action, you are putting yourself on the path to feeling strong and determined as an athlete. You are on the road to achieving. Through proper planning, and fostering relationships with supportive and wise people, you can create what you want.

As a final note, my athlete-clients tell me they post positive signs on their bedroom wall, powerful words from the Volition Mindset. Years later, the sign is still on their wall. They like it! It's cool to encourage yourself. No one else will see it—it's in your room. So if you want to do it, make a sign.

A suggested message would be:

I want to get stronger!

or

I will get stronger!

or

I'm Awesome!

Because you are.

Chapter 2
The Six Mental Skills

The Six Mental Skills at Your Service

There are six Mental Skills and they serve as the basic foundation in all sports to managing your thoughts, emotions, and behaviors. When athletes practice regularly, mental skills are incredibly powerful: They turn anxiety into calm, confusion into clarity, and doubt into confidence. Throughout this book, the skills are highlighted in stories, mindsets, and exercises. You'll read examples of athletes who are worried, stressed out, or very scared, but then they decide to shift into new thoughts and a different attitude. They learn to trust their abilities, speak positively to themselves, and play much better. When you train mentally, it's important to have a clear intention to practice often and apply the skills in the right moment. Use the skills every day to be able to overcome problems and enhance your moves. Just like studying in school, or being disciplined in sports, mental training is only successful when done frequently.

The Benefits

When you learn and practice mental skills, the benefits you will gain are:

- acute awareness of your thoughts, breath, and body,
- the capacity for deep focus, shutting out all distractions,
- the aptitude to slow down your mind, reduce stress and overcome struggles,
- accuracy and consistency in your performances,
- and the habit of creating a peaceful, confident inside even under pressure.

As you use these mental skills, you'll be able to execute in the most important moments and find that you truly believe in your abilities and in yourself. Both the skills and self-belief will guide you to feel bold in your performances.

6 MENTAL SKILLS

Breathing
to intentionally inhale and exhale fully,
producing a centered, calm mental & physical state

Relaxation
to breathe into and release muscle tension
to feel completely at ease

Positive Self-Talk
to speak aloud or silently to yourself,
using true positive statements, or repeating an
optimistic script to create an inner confidence

Recall
to relive an action in detail,
to flash back to a place or event,
or remember a personal feeling or thought

Visualization
to "dream" or imagine a performance;
to see in your mind's eye a certain place or event
and envision what you want to do

Concentration
to set your mind on one thing;
to sustain focus on one action at a time,
or a central image or thought

I learned these exact tools when I was fifteen years old, after a terrible accident in sports. I'm sharing the story with you, and perhaps you will understand my struggle, and how powerful mental training is...

The Crash: How I lost my skills, nearly quit, re-learned everything, and by a miracle won two National Titles

I was tumbling across the floor in the gym when it happened. I ran and did a round-off, flip-flop, punch! I jumped up in the air for a double back (two flips backwards). Suddenly, I got lost—was I in the first flip or the second flip? I opened up my position and wham! I crashed on the back of my head. My right knee slugged my forehead—whack! I was out.

I woke up after a minute, iced my head, and my coach called my mom and sent me home...

The crash was intense. My head hurt, the whole thing freaked me out. But worst of all...fear began to paralyze my mind. Back in the gym, my gymnastics skills became scary, unfamiliar, and started to vanish. While I was training to make the U.S. National Team, I found myself falling into a mental black hole. When it was my turn in practice, I stiffened up, balked, and got confused in mid-air. I started losing my skills. Days went by and it got worse; I was crying all the time. Like amnesia, I suddenly "forgot" how. I panicked and wept. I was out of control—and for a month, I deteriorated. Four weeks later, I couldn't do 70% of my skills. My coaches were frustrated and confounded. They yelled, "What's wrong with you?" I had no answer and felt stupid and humiliated. My mom couldn't help, either. I was beside myself, lost and afraid. It felt like I was worthless, a nothing, because I was not a gymnast anymore. I wanted to quit and nearly did. I told my mom one night, "I'm going to quit." She listened, patiently. She told me it was my choice. But then she said I needed to realize I wouldn't be a gymnast any more, no more pretty leotards, team sweats, no practice with my teammates, no traveling to competitions, no getting out of school early for early workouts...I'd have to take PE, too. I'd be—normal.

Normal? I never thought I was normal. I was a gymnast. What would I do? Who would I be? That unknown was even scarier than how I was going to get my skills back. Because, my identity, my life, was wrapped up in training and competing. That's who I was, an athlete, a gymnast.

So I went to the gym for a few days, struggled through practices doing basics, basics, basics. My spirit was low, but I was at the gym, trying. And then the craziest thing happened. A sport psychologist came into my life. Dr. Ken Ravizza was a professor at Cal-State Fullerton in 1979; he guided both the baseball and women's gymnastics teams at CSUF to win National Championships that year, through mental training. Dr. Ravizza took me on as a client and taught me the mental skills. And the head coach for the CSUF gymnastics team, Lynn Rogers, helped me in the gym. It was a little strange at first: Ken and I spent an hour in his office, talking, me feeling nervous at times, yet learning the tools: breathing, relaxing, positive self-talk, visualization, recall, and concentration. I wrote and took notes. I was quiet, sat still and studied. I also reflected on my practices, especially when I started to feel afraid. I recognized my negative thoughts and feelings and learned about myself. I learned about my fears, how and when I shut down, how to notice when the fear started, and how I could shift into new thoughts.

It was unfamiliar, sitting, talking, and writing to help me in gymnastics, but it really helped! I did repetitions of concentration drills and how to control my breath, my thoughts, and my body. I practiced visualizing and focusing on the smallest details of movement. Slowly, s-l-o-w-l-y, I came back. Like a two-year-old doing front rolls on the ground, I started over and re-learned my gymnastics skills in the gym with Ken and Lynn's encouragement. I trained and applied the mental tools, intensely, for three months: two hours a day, twice a week. It was very scary. Very. Scary. But I understood how to manage my fears. I mastered how to breathe out my tension. I attained a focus that guided my body to perform. And I got back to competition. It was the hardest thing in my life, and applying the tools in competition took practice…and patience… Through competition season, a few months later, I qualified to the 1980 Jr. Olympic National Championships.

The funny thing about that was three months prior, my mom had asked me what my goal was for the year. I joked. I said, "I'm going to win Nationals." And we both laughed. What a dream! But I practiced using the mental skills, and I centered my mind in meets. And when I got to Nationals, I saw great gymnasts, but I had learned to stay in tune with myself, and I hit all of my routines. Total surprise…I won! I won the USA Jr Olympic All-Around and Beam titles. After a horrible accident and mental breakdown, I became a 2-time National Champion.

How to Mentally Prepare for Challenges

Playing sports goes with facing challenges. The crash and the fear I went through were quite serious. Most athletes will not experience *that* level of mental stress and physical setbacks. It's rare. But all athletes get hurt, experience nervousness, and fight many other difficulties to be mentally prepared. And to have your most positive, strong mind, I'm introducing you to another mindset.

Mindset: Expectancy

Expectancy is the quality, or a state, of looking forward or anticipating what's next, or what may come in the near future. It's common for athletes to feel surprised, especially when they're not mentally prepared. To be alert and willing to handle any situation, these are important. Below is a quick lineup of what to expect when you play sports, and clear mindsets to meet challenges.

Adopting a system of expectant thoughts creates a sense of confidence, saying, "I'm ready!" and "I've got this!"

1. Expect to play your best. This is an extremely positive and assertive mentality—expect to do well. Understand that winning, losing, or being the best is not the focus: those are momentary and they are results. The focus is how you think, feel, and perform. In practice, if you think, "I'm not sure I can do it," then you likely will not do it. Do you want to give the game to your competitor? Say, "I will play hard," "I can do this," or "I'm going to do great!" These thoughts lead to positive and confident feelings.

2. Expect to face a tough competitor. When you underestimate your opponent, you underestimate preparing for a game. When you imagine a tough player or team, you will strategize beforehand and you will rise. Also, when you face a weaker competitor, expect to play hard and be respectful. Offer them a good challenge and improve your own game.

3. Expect mistakes and to be resilient. To have "perfect practices" or especially a "perfect game" is rare for any athlete. Mistakes happen. Athletes who recover quickly are eager and prepared. They seek to be positive and often overcome their opponent, no matter what.

4. Expect pain, sore muscles, and occasional tweaks or injuries. The body can take a lot, but sometimes you will hit full exhaustion and/or get hurt. Be ready to be responsible. Manage treatments with help from an adult, rest and take care of yourself. See chapter 10, "Body Smart," for tips.

5. Expect flat days, even setbacks in practice and performance. Advancing in sport is not a constant. Some days are off, or really off. When you're struggling, you may wonder, "What's going on?" or "Who's body is this?" It's okay, it's temporary. You can handle it. But if an athlete gets disappointed or angry because they're not doing great, they are only hurting themselves and possibly their team.

6. Expect harmony and disharmony. Plan on knowing and talking kindly with teammates, being supportive. Also understand that not everyone has a "buddy" or likes each other all the time. Emotions can be erratic in sports. Keep cool and stick to being calm and respectful toward each other.

7. Expect to follow rules and safety precautions. Even when an athlete disagrees, rules and preventative measures are created for good reasons, especially for the care of all participants. But if you cannot perform because of a rule's limitations, then it's important to politely inquire to your coach or parent.

8. Expect to be treated with dignity. Positive criticism is important. If you are subject to name-calling, or offensive or demeaning language, then you need to decide if that's the environment you want. Coaches and players can tear you down or build you up. If you can choose, then choose a favorable coach/team who treats you right.

9. Expect to be disciplined and make sacrifices. Go to practice, be on time, get plenty of sleep, and eat healthy foods for energy and recovery. Maybe you will miss TV shows or social time because of sports. Depending on your goals and/or team goals, you will decide how disciplined you want to be.

Challenges are No Match for a Higher Mind

If playing sports is a big part of your life, then so are challenges. The simple view is that challenges are only problems to solve. Your mind is intelligent. Your mind can create new thoughts and perform mental strategies! Your mind has the capacity to do amazing things. Believe it. So practice the Six Mental Skills, go out in the world and conquer the challenges!

Kick-butt Practices and Exercises for Chapter 2

Learn the Six Mental Skills

First, I will explain each skill, then give instructions, then direct you to do it.

Exercise: Breathing

What is it? To bring yourself into a state of focus, sureness, and calm control, it starts with breathing. Every moment of your day, you inhale and exhale to stay alive. That is involuntary breathing; it comes naturally. But intentional breathing is a skill to get centered in your body and get in tune with yourself so you can perform. I will remind you throughout this book to practice intentional inhaling and exhaling and take slow deep breaths. I call it the "4-8."

How to do it: Take a deep 4-count inhale through the nose. Inhale 1..2..3..4—fill yourself with air. Like a blown-up balloon, your belly and lungs are expanded. Hold for four seconds…then a very slow 8-count exhale out the mouth, 1..2..3..4..5..6..7..8… Your body deflates, goes limp, the balloon lets out all of its air, slowly. Breathing is central to your ability to calm and focus yourself.

Practice: Off the court, or just before playing, take three deep breaths before you perform. You can also breathe and rehearse in your mind the moves or race you want to have. At night, before bedtime, lie down and take five deep breaths and visualize how you want to perform. Make sure you let go of the day's issues and tension, first. Be ready to go into a "dream state." Settle your mind and body, do the deep breathing and see clearly your performance. If there are mistakes, let go and start again. Focus on the relaxed feeling you have in bed. See Chapter 7, "Visualize" to learn accurate visualization.

SLOW DEEEP BREATHING

INHALE 4 COUNTS 1, 2, 3, 4...
—hold 4 counts ~
EXHALE 8 COUNTS 1, 2, 3, 4, 5, 6, 7, 8...

Exercise: Relaxation

What is it? To breathe air into all body parts, then exhale and release tension, soften muscles to become heavy, loose, and feel at ease. To access a relaxed state at the right moment, this takes practice. And I know all athletes get tense!

How to do it: Lie down on your back, hands and feet apart, and put attention on different body parts, one at a time. Breathe in and out deeply, and on the exhale, release tension throughout the body; let go of muscle tension. Do a mental check of each major body part: neck, shoulders, arms, torso, hips, legs, feet…even your face. Talk to your body. Tell your muscles to relax, get heavy. For a sharp release, you can contract muscle groups, hold…then let go. For example, inhale and squeeze your hands tightly; then on the exhale, release them. Feel your hands relax. Next, inhale again, squeeze your hands and add your arms. Tense the arm muscles tightly on the inhale, then exhale slowly and soften your hands and arm muscles. Then add your shoulders…inhale and squeeze your hands, arms, and shoulders, then exhale and tell them to relax, feel them get heavy. Think of your jaw and mouth…part your lips, and tell your jaw to let go, feel it loosen. Go through each major body part, hands, arms, stomach, glutes, quads, hamstrings, lower legs, feet…squeeze on inhale, then release and relax on exhale.

Practice: It's important to relax for a few moments every day. For sports, match relaxing with inhaling and exhaling…on the sidelines, just before you perform. Also at night, before bedtime, take deep breaths and relax, loosen your muscles on the exhale. With practice, you can relax your entire body in a few seconds for free-flowing movement. Look up Progressive Relaxation. This teaches you the distinct difference between tense muscles…and a relaxed body. When you perform, you want to eliminate tension that causes stiff movements.

Exercise: Positive Self-talk

What is it? To speak to yourself aloud or silently, using true positive words or phrases.

How to do it: Sit down and write a list of true positive statements about you as a person and as an athlete. You know, your strengths and qualities. Five or more, like, "I am fast," or "I am strong," or "I work hard." Or thoughts like, I'm assertive, motivated, or friendly. If you have difficulty, ask a friend or family member what good things they see in you. Make a list.

Practice: Repeat these true statements to yourself every morning or night for a month, so the messages become natural to you. This is integral to connecting with yourself—to know who you are and what you are good at. This is not bragging; it boosts your confidence while speaking the truth. Positive words about yourself are very powerful and give you great energy!

Exercise: Recall

What is it? To Remember. Close your eyes, recall a successful play or move from practice, or a competition.

How to do it: See it in your mind two ways. 1) Audience Member: See yourself from a view that you're sitting in the stands, in the audience, and you can see yourself play, like you are watching a movie screen, so to speak, and you are in the movie playing sports. I call this "3rd Person." 2) Your View: See through *your* eyes, like you are *in your body*. This is a "1st Person" view. This is most powerful. Re-live your movements. *See* and *feel* your body's speed, style, and flow, every part, one moment at a time. Experience Recall, like a fabulous dream.

Practice: Do this nightly. Even at practice or a game, pause for 10-30 seconds and recall a good play you've done before. Feel clear about what that was like and repeat it again and again; up to ten times is not too much. Mental images of success will guide you in the present moment.

Exercise: Visualization

What is it? To Imagine what you want. This is like dreaming of a place, event, or performance; you can see snapshot images, slow motion movement, regular or at a fast pace.

How to do it: Close your eyes, imagine you're on a beach—blue sky. The bright sun is shining on your skin. You're sitting on a red and white striped towel in your bathing suit, toes in the sand…you can hear the waves rolling… Can you smell the salty air? Can you see the ocean? Visualizing creates pictures in your mind with sensory details; done in a positive manner, you can see what you want to do or accomplish. If you can see it, it becomes more real. It's just like a physical event. The brain recognizes it as real, and then, the more you visualize, you are focused on something good and very likely to make it happen!

Practice: Imagine performing a skill in your sport—a move or play. Imagine making a game-winning shot. Dream that you won and you're standing on the top of an award stand. See it. Feel it. Use your imagination. Practice each night in bed for a few minutes, and that will prepare you for the next day. Later, in Chapter 7, "Visualize, Visualize," learn how to break down skills into parts. You'll understand simple details about how your brain works when you pause, slow down, and notice accurate positions. This is one of the most powerful tools in mental training. Every time you visualize, you are starting to create exactly what you want.

Exercise: Concentration

What is it? To set the mind on one thing and sustain focus on it. Put your mind's attention on one thing at a time. Be in the present moment, immersed in only one thing. Right now.

How to do it: Look at your hands, your fingers, knuckles, and palms. Just look at them and study the lines, the colors, and shapes. Then think of your hands on a ball, the texture of the ball, soft, smooth, bumpy, and the size. Think about it. You are concentrating as you focus on just your hand, and your hand on a ball. When you tied your shoes for the first time, you had to do it many times, you had to look and concentrate on the strings, wrapping them around, pushing the string between the loops, through the hole, and tightening the bow… It wasn't easy. Were you thinking of pizza when you were tying your shoe? I doubt it. It was challenging so you only focused on the strings and what your fingers were doing. You need to apply that importance on your basic moves. Study your body and movement, one position at a time.

Practice: Think of a basic technical move in your sport, maybe a quick leg-muscle action, a powerful kick…think of the feel when you make hard contact, your foot strikes the ball. No thoughts of a past kick or future moment—just the present kick. Think only on what your body feels: your arms held out or swinging by your body—and what you see, your foot, the ball. Do it five times in your mind, kick, kick, kick, feel, feel, feel, see, see, see. Focus on the movement, focus…focus… As you slow down your mind for at least 5 minutes each day in practice or at home, recalling your technique, you are practicing concentration. This will increase your ability to be in tune with your body, shut out distractions, and to concentrate.

Growing Confidence and Self-Belief

'Confident' is what all athletes want to feel. When you practice these six mental skills, regularly, 4-5 days every week, you will definitely grow more confident over time. It's like brushing your teeth; if you brush twice a day, thoroughly, you'll have nice white teeth and fresh breath! Regular mental training gives you clear and confident thoughts, and you will readily believe in your inner strength and physical performances. That self-belief will make you soar!

Chapter 3

Master Inner Calm and Concentration

Find Inner Calm to Concentrate

When you are quiet and calm, it is much easier to concentrate.

Let me repeat that: When you are quiet and calm, it is *much* easier to concentrate. Plus, when a person finds their inner calm, a deeper state of concentration and higher performance are possible.

On the other hand, when you are agitated, very excited, or extremely nervous, thoughts run rampant and you're not in control. Otherwise known as 'mental chaos,' you feel distracted and tense and your performance suffers.

This chapter will help you understand different methods for becoming calm and focused. When you practice calmness, your intention becomes clear, you feel in control of your body, and you will play your best.

Some people think getting calm is just not talking. Or it's just sitting still. But there's much more to understanding calm, because it has parts.

Parts to Getting Calm

1. be still…
2. be quiet…
3. relax your muscles to feel peaceful…and
4. focus on the present moment.

But wait, that's not entirely easy. To focus on the present, you will need to release past events that are uncomfortable, and future events you want to avoid, because you can't control the past or the future. The only moment you can control is now.

One more time: The only moment you can control is now.

Consider my past incident—the crash on my head mentioned in Chapter 2. Thinking about the crash made me feel confused, upset, and afraid. To do gymnastics and be successful, I had to choose a new focus. I had to release past thoughts and future fears. I needed to focus and only think about the present moment because my mind was out of control, and bad thoughts of the crash were not helping me. In fact, it was distracting me and keeping me in the past. Future thoughts might be nice to daydream about at home, but while practicing and competing, you need your mind to be in the present moment, on your body and your breath, and your movements. What's happening right now. So I'd like to introduce a new mindset…

Mindset: Present-moment Awareness

Present-moment Awareness is being in tune with your body's position, movement, and your thoughts and breath as it's happening. It's being focused on yourself, now; not in the past, not in the future, not what your mom just said, and not what your coach *will* say. Just what is happening with you right now.

The benefit of using present-moment awareness is that you'll possess the ability to get calm and manage pressures, distractions, worries, doubts, and fears. As you focus on the present moment, your mind only takes in what you are doing right now. In a practice or game, you don't worry about a past kick or move, you don't think about the future results—success or failure—you simply stay with yourself in the moment. If you are on the sidelines or waiting for a turn, you can pause and get still and quiet. Start noticing your breath…inhaling and exhaling…Get calm by focusing on your breath, slowly moving in and out of your body and notice how you feel.

In any situation, it is you and only you who decides what you think about. So when you practice present-moment awareness, you can notice air filling up your lungs, and the air going out of your body. In this way, you're doing a self-study. You are aware of your breath and your body's soft motion. Notice how your chest and abdomen rise on the inhale…then sink and fall slowly on the exhale. Get in tune with how your hands and arms feel right now. Become aware of your body being calm in the present moment. This awareness will increase a peaceful, confident feeling inside…and your ability to concentrate.

Jittery, anxious, and trying too hard

Ben Peters is a golfer. When we met, he had never qualified to a major golf tournament, just local ones. And he'd never travelled by plane for one, either. When I asked what his goal was, he said, "I want to go pro." He fully believed he had the talent, but he was inconsistent in his game, and would suddenly fold under his own pressure when he was doing well.

I came to know Ben over many months as we worked together on preparation for his strokes and putts. I taught him how to be aware of his thought patterns and ways to shift his overall mindset. He's a great guy, a friendly guy, and super fun! He loves to joke around in a lighthearted way. When describing himself on the golf course with other players, he said he hopes everyone is having a good time, not being overly critical or serious. And…he hopes the other golfers like him in return.

Well, of course, who doesn't want to be liked? We all want that.

But Ben went out of his way to be more aware of the other players than focusing on his own mental game. When it came time for his shot and advancing his level of play, Ben worried what others thought and he tightened up. He got nervous, tried too hard, and took it way too seriously.

He was distracted. He doubted his abilities. And he certainly wasn't having fun.

I told him during a session in my backyard, "You need to get in tune with yourself, Ben. It seems you are tense on the golf course. The skill you need to master is calmness. We're going to practice being still, quiet, and relaxing your muscles so you can connect to your body and movements. You need to let go of what others might think and increase awareness of yourself." He agreed he needed that. So we stood up, and I showed him how to inhale through his nose: four counts, filling himself up with air…then I exhaled slowly out of my mouth for eight counts, softening my shoulders, neck, face, and whole body. We stood there, still, and quiet…We practiced that together three times, and Ben started to feel a sense of peace as he focused on his breathing. His body and mind relaxed in the moment. This was a new experience for him. He was slowing down, letting go of tension, and getting in tune with the present moment.

"This is helpful!" he said.

Great. I told him he needs to practice this every day. Especially before he walks onto the golf course, he needs to take three, slow, deep breaths, and make sure to exhale all the way out. I told him, "This grounds you in your body, and it will remind you to be in tune throughout your practice or game." He liked that.

The next issue was being distracted by other golfers then tightening up. So we talked about the fact that he can't control the other players: what they think or say or do. He only has control over himself—his breath, his thoughts, his body—and he needs to focus on those things.

I asked, "You're coming to me for help, and you want to play pro…So, what's most important to you—that you get along with the other golfers, or that you play your best game?" "Play my best game," he said.

Okay, we had already gone over and over Ben's golf stroke. He broke it down and scripted it step-by-step, how he would hold his club, position his arms and feet, and move through the stroke—how it would feel like a smooth shot. Now, it was all about ease. Creating a calm, fluid, physical state—a mental image of fun, and not being so serious. Because when an athlete is enjoying what they're doing, they experience a sense of calm. When they are relaxed, they can focus better and they *will* perform better.

I reminded Ben about present-moment awareness—not thinking of the shot before, and not what someone might think after, just the present moment. He can notice his own breath and body and enjoy the game.

I sent Ben off to think about what is fun for him. Why does he like golf? And what makes him smile?

When he came back for the next session, Ben shared a story. He was golfing with a friend and, even though he loves being out on a beautiful green course under the blue sky, he found himself trying too hard to improve his shots. He felt tense and he knew it. At one of the holes, he turned and saw a group of young kids on a grassy hill, off to the side of the course. The kids at the top of the hill grabbed hands, and altogether, they ran down the hill giggling and laughing and screaming with joy, having the time of their lives. That looked like fun. Ben looked at his friend and said, "You want to hold hands and run down a hill? Come on, it'll be fun." His friend began laughing, and the two of them finished their golf game totally relaxed. Ben shot very well, and he recognized his ability to get calm. He simply did the steps: he took a breath, relaxed, and shifted his thoughts from trying too hard, to just letting go and playing the game.

Weeks went by and he continued to use awareness. Ben practiced and applied the mental skills, and he kept seeing improvements in his demeanor and his game.

Months later, Ben won his first tournament. He said he was calm the whole time. He took moments to be still and quiet, he did the breathing and relaxing, and he stayed in tune with his body throughout the game. This was a pivotal day for him, experiencing his own mental strength and performing very well. Not long after that day, Ben qualified for the first time in his life to a major tourney: the U.S. Mid-Amateur in Pennsylvania. He got on a plane...I cried with happiness.

Who knows, maybe Ben will go pro someday, or maybe not. But what Ben *is* doing, he is 'playing' golf better than he ever did before.

Notice Your Thought Patterns

Like Ben, all athletes get caught up in their own crippling thoughts: distracting thoughts of opponents, not wanting to be judged, worrying about missing a shot, a kick, or failing, and the most common problem is criticizing yourself.

To manage your thoughts, you need to recognize them and your patterns. You need to become aware of *yourself*.

STOP FIGHTING YOURSELF!

Self 1 vs. Self 2

"Oh, that was bad!" "Man, I'm slow," "God, I'm nervous," "What am I doing here?" "What's wrong with me—run faster!" "I don't think I can do this…"

Let me introduce you to *yourself*—your critical voice—also known as Self 1. In the book, *The Inner Game of Tennis* by W. Timothy Gallwey, he says we all have a judgmental, doubting, and bossy voice. I agree! Self 1 is your critical voice that does not prompt inner calmness or sureness. It is hard on you when you make mistakes. It doesn't forgive. And it is not objective. Your critical voice tightens you up and holds you back—totally prevents you from feeling relaxed and confident, and truly hurts your performance.

But there is great news, Gallwey continues, there's also Self 2! Self 2 is your body. The Do-er, the Performer. Your body is smart, really smart. But your body's intelligence is often overpowered by Self 1. Learning to notice and be aware of your critical voice and let go of self-criticism is a skill. When you get in tune with your body, Self 2 is the key to best execution. When you connect with your physical body and breath, then see and feel your movement, and trust your body's abilities, you will thrive. But it takes awareness, attention to thought and body, and a calm mind and clear approach.

Mr. Gallwey is genius for developing the philosophy and tactics of Self 1 and Self 2. Thank you! Every athlete can distinguish between them by noticing and practicing, and the first step is to get quiet, get calm, and become aware of your inner voice. Study your thinking habits, how you've been programmed with negativity and doubts. Then...you can adjust.

Common negative thoughts:

I can't get my shot straight.

I'm slow. I'm not good enough.

My coach keeps yelling at me.

I'm nervous about the game; I don't want to lose.

My parents keep bothering me about homework and cleaning my room.

My friends are ignoring me.

My teacher is terrible; she doesn't explain what will be on the test.

Okay, you can't control your parents, coach, or anyone, but you can control your own thoughts. Negative thoughts can become a habit, and habits are hard to break. I wonder: How do you want to feel? Do you want to feel in control? Do you want to feel powerless...or powerful?

The key factor to being in control and feeling powerful is that your thoughts are energy, and your high, or low, energy thoughts often lead to *feelings*.

Thoughts are Energy and Thoughts Lead to Feelings

Quickly, did you know that your thoughts vibrate? They do! It's a universal law: the Law of Vibration. Through science, we know everything in the universe has energy. Everything you see around you moves or vibrates with energy: people, animals, plants, trees, they all vibrate at a certain frequency. Even you. You vibrate with energy at different levels in relation to your thoughts.

So, if you want to have high energy, think positive thoughts: "I'm going to make this shot," "I am fast!" These thoughts actually raise your vibration frequency in your body and give you higher energy. Adversely, negative thoughts produce low levels of vibration. Negative thoughts lead to low energy, which leads to poor performance. If you want to perform your best, think good thoughts!

Thoughts —› Lead —› to Feelings

Okay, what type of energy do you want to have?

Since your emotions directly affect your performance, remember, every single thought you have is energy. Your thoughts activate emotion inside you. Negative thoughts create tension, nervousness, anxiety, doubt. Thoughts of being relaxed and focused give you a calm feeling. Positive, happy thoughts give a sense of ease, physical power, and optimism!

Examples:

Thoughts		Related Feelings
My dog is sick	>>>	sad, worried
I fell in competition	>>>	frustrated, angry
My birthday party is coming	>>>	excited
My friend makes me laugh	>>>	happy
I will do well in my game	>>>	determined
I keep my eye on the ball	>>>	focused
I am ready…breathe and relax	>>>	calm and confident

If you want to feel confident, thoughts matter! Think of what you want to do, and remind yourself of your positive qualities. If you want to rise, then don't downplay your strengths and abilities. Don't be modest or shy. Connect your mind to your positive spirit and the power inside you.

The Quiet Power Inside You

Are you aware of your quiet inner power? As an athlete, you experience your physical movement and power all the time. But inside your mind, you have a still, silent strength that has amazing potential. It's your quiet mind that listens…and thinks…and it's your own voice. It takes real intention to "plug in" and let it be your guide. The main obstacles are external distractions—you are attached and influenced by your coach's power, or friend's, or parents' power; and there are internal distractions—your thought patterns have been programmed to react to outer voices and opinions. The key is to get quiet and go inside yourself to listen to your own thoughts.

To be in tune with yourself is not always natural. It takes practice to become aware. When you feel stopped, trapped, or unable to move forward, it's helpful to be reminded of your inner power. My mom did that for me. She always reminded me that I have the strength inside me, and that helped me tremendously in creating positive thoughts, how I approached sports and overcame injuries and challenges. When my mom wasn't with me, I was with me. I talked to myself. I have thoughts and a voice!

You do have a quiet inner power. You can choose your thoughts. You can turn a difficult practice into a better one. You can get calm anywhere and let your calmness lead you.

Decide to get calm before, during, and after practice

Top athletes intentionally take a breath before entering the gym or court. They center themselves. When you want to concentrate, it's important to calm yourself with a breath, first. You can take a breath as you tie your shoes, as the coach speaks, or just before the game whistle. Take a breath before you shoot a free-throw or get on the starting block. Take a breath after a big play. In order to focus, get calm.

Why breathe? Because it brings awareness to your body, alleviates agitation, and a slow deep breath gives you a peaceful and centered feeling. It also reduces stress. From this quiet mental and physical state, you will feel more control over your mind and body. Using the four methods to get calm—be still, quiet, relax your muscles, and focus on the present moment—is the opposite of chaos and confusion. Getting calm helps you to be aware and in charge of your body. You will feel in control while you breathe, which hushes your nervous energy and promotes flow in your movement. But if you don't practice, it won't happen when you want it to.

My golf client, Ben, practiced getting immersed in the present moment. He learned to let go of attachments—needing others to like him, needing to win. During his golf game, as he practiced taking a breath and relaxing before each shot, he actually performed *better*. He didn't rush. He didn't try too hard. He became still and quiet in the moment. For a faster sport, like basketball or soccer, you can find moments in between plays, or on the sidelines, to take a breath and calm yourself.

At the end of your sports practice, you can really slow down and get calm. It's a great time to mentally rehearse being in control and accurate. Because you are closely connected to the physical moves you just executed and are trying to perfect. You are thinking how you want to make your moves better. So that's the time to create the image of playing or competing the way you want. After a hard practice, that's the best time to get calm by being still and quiet and relaxing…and concentrating. Even for 5 minutes, this is very beneficial, and it feels great! This practice of getting calm is also confidence-building. You can close your eyes (sitting or lying down) and surrender all of your energy to visit your own mind. Relive what went well and make the corrections you desire. Mental training is calculating each thought and physical act. Getting calm and imagining yourself playing your best will give you assurance and poise.

Consider when you are a passenger in the car ride home, you can "nap" in a dream world of your own. Get calm and imagine your best plays, your sharpest moves, your fastest race. If you can see it in your mind, you are imprinting the success to come. When you see it over and over, and it's real in your mind, you are more likely to achieve it!

Safe Peaceful Place

An excellent calming method is to envision or recall a place you like. Seeing in your mind's eye a wonderful place can also calm your energy, and this sets a tone to visualize your best performance.

Your mind is so powerful, you can imagine a beautiful, comfortable, or far-away place. You can pretend you are at the beach, in a forest, on an African safari with elephants, or just in your cozy bed with fluffy pillows and blankets. In addition to words and messages, images trigger emotions and energy, too. With an image of a place, you can generate excited, anxious, or soothing feelings.

Where do you feel the most peaceful and safe? Think about it, and as you see it in your mind, use this 'place' as a familiar image you can think of any time or anywhere. When I ask my clients where they feel most peaceful and safe, many athletes say, "My bed." Others say, "My room," or "The ocean," or "Out in nature."

Think of your safe peaceful place. Can you see it? Imagine you are
there now. See colors, shapes, hear sounds, notice smells. If it's the
ocean air, you're at the beach. Hear the waves, the birds flying over. See and feel
the warm sun shining down.

I've sketched a picture of my peaceful spot. I grew up close to the beach, so it's
my safe peaceful place! I love imagining I'm at the ocean; it really soothes my
mind and spirit.

I encourage you to practice seeing your own peaceful place when you lie down
and breathe deeply and relax. You can draw or paste a picture that is peaceful.
When you imagine your place, this is a great starting point to visualize your
sports performance.

Mental Training at the University of Utah

A few years ago, I asked some of my teammates from Utah, "How did we win Nationals so many times?" Because it is amazing—six National Championships in a row. Each of them answered, "It was Dr. Henschen and mental training."

Our team sport psychologist was Dr. Keith Henschen. In addition to regular gymnastics practice, we had an ongoing schedule to meet with him, listen to him, share our thoughts, and do mental exercises. At the end of practices, Dr. Henschen strolled into the gym with his long legs and big smile and gathered us in a circle. He was so laid back. He laughed and teased us in a playful way that made us relax.

There were two major areas we focused on: 1) to have team unity through communication and trust, and 2) to execute excellent performances in competition. Dr. Henschen got us to open up. We shared our deepest thoughts and feelings; we were honest with each other and trusted each other. It was important to have mutual respect, be completely authentic, and feel like a family. Because when you're closely connected, your group-emotions can elevate you to train hard, get through the tough stuff, and win.

To be able to physically perform our best, Dr. Henschen guided us through mental training exercises to manage our internal messages and images. He told us to lie down in a comfortable position on a mat; lying on our backs, hands and feet uncrossed. He played a tape of a tranquil voice, prompting us to inhale slowly, then exhale all the way out, releasing all the tension in our muscles. We got calm. We also did progressive relaxation—one major body part at a time, tightening it, then relaxing it—until our entire bodies were completely at rest. The tense-relax exercise got us in tune. We became acutely aware of our physical state. We learned the distinct difference of our muscles clenched tight…and then softened. While being quiet and focused on myself, I learned excellent body awareness and control.

At rest, lying on the mats, we sailed into our own mental worlds…we listened to soft music and visualized our skills and routines, one by one. Nothing else existed… In my mind, I imagined…and dreamed excellent moves…and I often fell asleep. Dr. Henschen said, "If you fall asleep, that's fine. It's your body talking to you, and it's exactly what you need."

The best part was feeling relaxed while doing gymnastics in my mind. I was in my own world, practicing confidence and accuracy. And Henschen also gave us meet strategies—to pre-plan what we would do every moment in between performances: help a teammate, move a mat, do a team cheer, or get quiet and visualize. Every moment was planned. I took time to relax and visualize, every day. With regular mental training, we were able to perform under pressure at the right moment…and win.

If You want to Win, Increase Concentration

How can athletes increase concentration? To achieve sustained focus with distractions all around, an athlete needs to slip into their own world and block out everything else. It takes volition, a strong, disciplined desire to practice being quiet, and focusing your thoughts on the task at hand.

Visit your inner world, then decide to stay there. When you're not
playing well, negative thoughts easily come, and it's common to defeat yourself. The crucial decision is to reconnect to what you want. Think of your desire: *I want to throw straight. I want to make this pass. I want to push off my foot and jump higher.* Also, disconnect from outside distractions: a voice, a sound, talented players, or movement around you that does not help you. Get immersed into your breath and body instead. Refocus by talking to yourself like an encouraging coach: "Come on, you can do this." Then repeat instructions or cues to focus on your body being accurate, fast, or graceful. Remember, your inner voice is a guide for you.

When practicing or playing, decide to stop judging yourself as good or bad. Remember, Self 1: the critical voice, is not helpful. Accept the process in sports, all the ups and downs. Judgment takes away from concentration, and it makes sense that some days are better and others are not; when they're not, you will try your best.

Focus on the facts, not judgment. No emotion, just positive corrections. This helps with concentration—to focus on simple facts. Use a wise voice, not a critical one: "I need to stretch out my arm in my stroke," "I want to extend my leg more," "I was soft on my take-off; I need to push harder off my right foot."

To regulate your mind and body in a balanced state of concentration, inhale and exhale, take a second to release muscle tension and center yourself by getting calm. Think about your body's position and movement, before, during, and after a play. Repeat the mental image and flow of the performance you want to have, what it feels like. Continue to speak positive words to yourself and encourage yourself. This is concentration.

Reduce Outer World Distractions

Distractions like phones, apps, social media, and the internet can be the most common and worst interference with improving concentration. Your mind leaps around here and there, taking quick pit-stops into other people's voices, messages, and pictures. You end up comparing your life to theirs, their looks to yours, and then you want to dive in and respond. This won't help you. This is confusion, disorder, and fleeting amusement. If you want to improve in sports, consider where to put your time and energy. Ask, what does a champion ponder? Where do they put their mind? I suggest you reduce screen time. If texting is a continual habit, then that seems like a distraction. Don't you think? Posting or looking at "fun" pics on Instagram, eh. Better to choose a role model to influence you. Like the best coaches or athletes in the world—those people and those messages directly relate to your goals, yes? And they may even inspire!

Write to Increase Concentration—Your Mental Training Notebook

The sharpest concentration is when you are clear in your mind and your thoughts are organized. You can do this best when you write it down in a notebook. From your brain to your hand to the page, writing can provide a focus for your mind.

Writing is concrete; it's solid. You see it with your eyes, and you feel the pen and notebook in your hands. You can pour out your thoughts and actions, track your journey and look back at what you've accomplished, or what you want to change. It's an act of personal power to write goals and the dates you want to achieve them. You can document your desires, strategies, and objectives. Record plans, use stickers. This can be fun! You can shop for a special notebook. It will be your Mental Training notebook or journal. Get a great color or design you like.

This 'book' is like your new best friend. Make weekly notes. Spend a few minutes with it every night. Write down what you want in big letters. Doodle or draw pictures if you like. You can paperclip nice cards or notes from someone else inside the pages. Create your notebook to suit your personality and interests, and keep it handy; keep it in the same place in your room.

When a person logs their thoughts and information in a notebook, they are increasing their focus on what they want to do. You're not just showing up for practice. You're not just following the coach's directions. You are producing your own inner world and dreams. You're leading yourself and building a mental focus. Check off goals when you reach them, and write a new one. This will give you momentum to keep reaching for what you want.

Speak to Yourself to Increase Concentration

Repeat to yourself what you want to achieve. Talk to yourself in the mirror. When you look at yourself and hear your own voice, you are deepening your memory and desire. When you share your goals with someone, it can increase your excitement as they support you. Talking about your efforts and progress is also courageous! Say what you want to achieve, tell someone, and declare it. This should be fun. It's not bragging or acting overly confident. You are a vibrant spirit with positive energy. As you speak, you are increasing personal power. This energy will help you to "zoom in" quicker in practice and in games and sustain confidence with deeper concentration.

For Teams and Individual Athletes

Mastering calm and concentration takes months and years of practice; these are learned skills. When you plan to improve your sports mind, your game will also improve. Whether you are an individual athlete or part of a team, you can practice on your own with the exercises in this book. Or if your coach, or a mental skills professional, suggests an exercise to enhance your concentration, it's great to practice with your team, like I did. Spend at least 5 minutes every day getting calm and concentrating on your mental game. Imagine. Believe in yourself. You can do it!

★ Kick-butt Practices and Exercises for Chapter 3 ★

Exercise: What *can* you control on your path to achieving your goals?

· See the illustration of the mountain on the next page; focus on the human figure at the top, arms up high. That's you.

· You climbed the mountain! Next to you (the small person at the top) write: "I did it!"

· A climber brings a pack of supplies, so you will bring "things" you can control.

· Review the word list provided.

· Write down the words that you believe you *can* control; write them on the left side of the mountain, going upwards. For example, breathing. Who controls your breathing? Someone else…your mom, your brother, or you? I'm gonna give this to you: it's you. You control your breathing, so that is in *your* control and you can write it on the left side of the mountain.

· All the things you *can* control, you take with you up the mountain. If an item does not apply to you, like college stuff, then omit. Leave them out.

· When you know 100% that you can *not* control something or someone, then cross it out. You do *not* take those up the mountain. You let them go. Feel clear and good letting go of what you *can't* control, and clear and good about what you *can* control.

Thoughts	Finishing homework	~~Opponents / Competitors~~
Feelings	Participating in family activities	~~Parents' thoughts / Words / Rules~~
Anxiety		
Nervousness	Respecting yourself	~~Others' expectations~~
Breathing	~~Supervisor / Advisor / Boss~~	~~Coach / Teammates~~
Communication	~~The Lottery~~	~~Officials / Judges~~
Actions	Respecting others	Living healthy lifestyle
Decisions	Extra workouts	Colleges you apply to
Hours you Sleep	Athletic field / Court / Gym	~~Colleges that accept~~ you
Food intake	~~Weather~~	~~Dog / Cat / Hamster / Pet~~
Texting / Online chats	~~Getting Injured~~	~~The President of the United States~~
Social time with friends	Caring for Injuries	
	Time / Clock	

Helpful tip: If you think to yourself, *I can't control my thoughts*…I understand.

It *seems* that way. But you are the only one who truly decides what you want to think about. Because your dad doesn't control what you think, does he? Or a coach…does your coach control your thoughts? I don't think so.

And you may wonder, do I control whether I get injured? Usually, not. Often, it's an accident. But you can be careful and do preventative care by treating sore muscles and swollen ankles at home. Most important, understand that no one else has power over you or your thoughts. You decide.

Exercise: Warm Washcloth

You experience many things through your senses: you see, hear, smell, taste, and touch. You may often feel comforted in a cocoon of warm blankets, or relaxed with the warm sun on your skin, maybe holding someone's hand. To feel touch and warmth gives us comfort. To stimulate that soothing feeling, and to practice a solitary moment being peaceful, you can connect your mind to a relaxing experience. This is a way to continue to train your mind and rid tension that blocks your best performance.

1. Soak a washcloth in hot water, get it nice and hot

2. Squeeze out and place hot washcloth in a bowl near a place you can rest

3. Lie down, take a few deep breaths, relax your muscles throughout your body

4. Think of a safe peaceful place for 1 minute.

5. Place the warm washcloth on your face, leave space to breathe

6. For 3-5 minutes, enjoy the warm sensation, breathe slowly, and imagine your safe peaceful place. Take deep breaths. You may also imagine walking in nature.

Exercise: Dump Negative Thoughts

Get negative thoughts out. To focus on positive things, empty your mind of worries and frustrations, first.

1. Grab paper and pen, or get your Mental Training notebook.

2. Write down worries and distracting thoughts (3–5 items or more). Things bothering you, including school, family, or any pressure. If something feels like a distraction, get it out. These negative thoughts are mental obstacles and do *not* help you concentrate or perform.

3. After writing down your items, you may dispose of the list. You can cross out the list with dark lines or X's. Or you can crumple it up tight, fist it in your hand, and throw it away! Throw your worries in the trash—get rid of them! Worries are mental garbage and you can regularly dispose of them.

4. Now, you dumped your mental garbage. What will you choose next? How about positive thoughts.

Exercise: Fill Your Mind with Positive Thoughts

Now, time to fill your mind with what you want. You recently emptied out the negative thoughts. Now, re-focus and create helpful, positive thoughts.

1.   Write on paper or in your notebook, a list of technical corrections or other things you *want* to achieve.

Examples of positive desires:

   I want to relax on my swing.

   I want to have tight form on my dives.

   I want to break 5 minutes on my run.

   I want to focus on technique and make 100 shots, today.

2.   Repeat your positive thoughts. Say what you want to do in front of your mirror, or to someone who is supportive.

These are specific positive thoughts and actions that guide you. You are becoming mentally stronger when you're clear about what you want to do, how you want to perform. You have the power. Create plans and intentions. Be distinct…then your mind is focused on affirmative action.

Exercise: Simple Body Awareness-Body Scan, Get in Tune with yourself

Practice *focus* by being in tune with your body. You can do this solo, or if someone can guide you through this exercise with their calm voice, that is helpful.

1.   In a quiet place, stand or lie down. When you get good, you can do this in seconds at practice or a game.

2.   Close eyes, breathe deeply and slowly 5 times.

3.   Put your attention on each body part, one at a time: focus on your hands and fingers…

4.   Take a breath, talk to your body and release tension, let go of any tightness.

5.   Focus on your arms…shoulders, chest, and abs…etc. Take a breath, let go…

6.   Go throughout your body, focus on each part and relax it.

7.   Notice your entire being feeling calm.

This Body Scan emphasizes concentration on you and your body. It can take 3 minutes at most. You are not tensing up at all. You are noticing and relaxing. When you do body scans, you are solely focused on your physical being, nothing else. This is excellent mental practice.

Exercise: Say Positive True Statements

Many athletes and coaches underestimate the power of words. But when you talk to yourself, it's most powerful. You need positive self-talk.

What has a parent, friend, teammate, or coach said to you that is a compliment? You're fast, you're strong, you work hard…What have they said? Their statements are true, yes?

You need to say these positive, true messages to yourself with your voice. Remember, you are the most important person you will communicate with for your entire life.

1. Write 3 Positive True Statements about yourself. Such as, I am strong. I work hard. I train mentally. Or I'm a good friend. I'm responsible. Anything that is true and positive.

2. Read out loud 5 times. Remember, this is *not* bragging. This is identifying your strengths and practicing concentration on yourself, instead of other distracting thoughts.

3. Practice saying these positive statements each day in front of your mirror. It may feel funny at first, talking to yourself, but again, be brave, take a risk, go after what you want.

Plain and simple, you are concentrating on you. Your brain is actively thinking, reading, and saying positive words that interact with your physical being. This mental exercise lifts your body's energy levels, and increases belief and focus on you.

Your Incredible Inner Power

It's empowering to know how your mind and body work together. None of these exercises will quickly change you into a calm, brave, confident athlete, or instantly improve concentration. It takes regular training—at least 60 days. When you practice, you will feel a change in your ability to get calm and focus on yourself. Your body's energy will also rise to perform your best. When you think and talk to yourself in a positive manner, you arouse your physical state. You stimulate a sense of incredible inner power, like a Superhero—if you can imagine that. And with this real, effective mind-power, you can increase focus and perform…superbly. Bet on it.

Chapter 4

Inner Strength, Values, and Gratitude

Have you ever felt invincible? You know, that incredible energy when you're on your game, you're super confident, powerful, fast, you can't miss, and you feel like you can do anything? I've experienced it. It's one of the most amazing feelings in sports! But for most athletes it's rare, especially to do this with frequency — to play with such fearlessness and move with such precision— yet, it is attainable. So the question is, where does "it" come from? And how can you achieve it more often?

For sure, physical preparation is necessary, but all athletes do that. Mental training is the next biggest key; practicing daily and using the mental tools certainly gives you a giant leg up. The other factor is another "soft tool" that is enchanting. It's a detail that coaches don't coach, and it's based on neuroscience and positive psychology. It is a very personal idea, a belief about yourself, that allows you to perform your best. It does not relate to sports at all…it relates to hugging…and being happy.

The Love Class

There were a hundred students in this class, and I promise you we couldn't wait to get there. Our fabulous professor was an energetic woman, who was also smart, bold, and full of passion. She was a retired nun who, for many years, taught prison inmates—this was an interesting woman! To be clear, the Love Class was the nickname; it was a human behavior class in psychology, and it was the most popular class on campus.

Beginning with the first day, our wise professor stood in front of us and smiled, "Hello, everyone. This is the Love Class, welcome. Your textbook is *Love* by Leo Buscaglia." She held up a small red paperback book that read, *Love*. "Please buy it and bring it tomorrow. Now, I'm not a rules person, but I do have two. Number one, you need to get 12 hugs a day… You think I'm kidding. I'm not. You can get two hugs in here, every day. The others, you will seek out in the world. So stand up, everyone, stand up. Introduce yourselves and hug someone!"

The entire class giggled, eyebrows were raised, but in a second, there was a huge hug-fest in the classroom. Bodies paused, names were exchanged, then students embraced with lots of talking and laughing.

"Okay, okay, you can sit down… Rule number two, in front of your mirror every day, you will say, 'I'm Terrific!'" Her fist shot up in the air. "This is very important. Do you know why?"

We waited…

"Because you will forget! And you can't wait for someone to remind you…Let's stand up and practice, now."

Apparently, she was serious, and she made sense. I do forget I'm terrific.

We all stood up. And despite my own inhibition to shout out 'I'm terrific' in front of a large classroom, I thought, okay, I think I can do this.

"Ready, and—" she started.

"I'm Terrific!" everyone said, half-heartedly. This was not natural.

"Ohhh, you can do better than that," she said. "Again!"

We gathered more courage, took a deep breath… "I'm Terrific!!!" Everyone vibrated.

Wow, the voices! This was invigorating. Big grins spread across faces, my body buzzed, and I got that bubbly high-on-life feeling. And even though it was slightly embarrassing, it was really cool. I felt so good inside, hugging, smiling, and shouting with a group of people I didn't know. It was like we were becoming friends right there on the spot, and we instantly liked each other. And more importantly, we liked ourselves. And *that* is something.

This story illustrates an important point. With your own personal power, you can create high emotion. Specifically, self-esteem, or, self love. Each student produced that amazing feeling of inner joy. In sports, this emotion is vital. Vi-tal! But not typically promoted in regards to working hard and reaching goals. Excitement and self-esteem: these are considered the *result* after the achievement. You like yourself more *after* you win, right? But the findings in positive psychology studies show very strong evidence for the flip-side. Happiness fuels success! The brain functions at a higher level—it is more focused, creative, motivated, and resilient. Accomplishments occur more often when emotions align with being cheerful and appreciating yourself.

The bottom line is that you need to increase your energy to play sports. To perform your best requires extraordinary thoughts and inner strength.

I learned in the Love Class that I form my thoughts; I generate my emotions, and I create my life. And you can, too. When you nurture your spirit and care for your emotional well-being, you are establishing a positive mental pattern. Let's go over that again: When you nurture your spirit, when you love yourself, you are establishing a critical, positive mental pattern. You are being your best…you are being mindful. Let me introduce you to a new mindset: Mindfulness.

Mindset: Mindfulness

Mindfulness is to put your attention on personal experiences, moment-by-moment, accepting them without judging 'good' or 'bad.' You are aware of your thoughts, emotions, and bodily experiences. You consider the details of your interaction with others, listening fully, considering how you want to speak and act. To practice, notice and stay in the present moment and accept what is happening.

Short List on Inner Strength…

Inner strength is key to achieving what you want, especially tackling those agonizing practices—the painful ones that accost you and make you shake and cry. When you face doubts and negative talk or there's intense pressure in a game, you *need* inner strength. Your mind is the core factor to create that. Top athletes around the world have that tough internal voice and determination. In addition to physical training, you must develop *you*. You need to be rooted in yourself, your knowledge, pursuits, and your beliefs. And in order for you to be your strongest inside, you need to pursue four personal disciplines.

1. Self-knowledge & Self-love

Know yourself—your habits, interests, values, best abilities, areas to improve, and your own self-talk. This is not simple, because we are distracted humans. We are influenced by others. But learn about who you are as a person, as an athlete. Write down what you like and love about yourself. What you want to improve on. With this knowledge, you will be a rock for yourself and others. You will honor and care about yourself. And from this place—you will feel more confident being connected to truth.

2. Surround Yourself with Positive People & Things

A very wise philosopher advised: Imagine yourself surrounded with the conditions you wish to achieve. I say, surround yourself, now. Keep company with wise, loving people, and voices. Choose individuals who make you feel good! People you admire, who nurture your growth. Listen only to positive words, positive criticism that moves you to be your best. Be intentional and place motivating items around you. Put up signs, posters, cards, pictures, little items around your room or in your locker or on a mirror — things that inspire you. Messages that remind you that you are fabulous, that you can get through tough times. Little statues or animals that make you feel good. Surround yourself, because these people and items are so important! And fun, too!

3. Actively Learn

When you take action, you are pursuing what's important to you. Identify skills or interests you want to learn more. Like, improve flexibility, speed, strength, game strategies; special interests, music, art, science; fun activities, maybe nature, skateboarding, drawing; goals to achieve, learning new skills, advancing to a higher level, making an all-star team. Keep learning! Take steps every week to learn through doing. Write out short plans in a notebook or on a calendar: stretch hamstrings and quads, 10 min. Whatever it is! Write it down. Tell friends and family what you are doing. Make this real and part of your daily life.

Learn. Do. Learn. Do. This process makes you feel alive!

4. Develop your Core Values

Core Values are a set of personal beliefs or philosophies. Do you always want to follow someone else's philosophies, or do you want to create your own? Think about it. You may be young, but you're smart, and by thinking about what's important to you, and knowing your core values, you can make clear choices on how you want to speak and act every day. You make decisions on what is most important in order to feel good about yourself as a person. You consider how you want to make an impact in this world. The more courageous you are in believing and practicing your core values, the stronger and more confident athlete, and person, you will be.

What You Value Most

Who do you want to be in this world? What is important to you? Kindness, respect, patience, teamwork? When you make choices, you can think of your values. If honesty or authenticity is meaningful to you, then be yourself completely. Don't hide. Or if it's kindness, then perhaps you can say kind words or be more helpful to others. Kindness is experienced through actions, and yet sincere, kind words can also give someone a wonderful feeling.

There is an exercise with Values at the end of this chapter, but for now you can ponder… Which values lead you to becoming the best athlete and give you a sense of self-respect? Hard work, discipline, excellence? Which values make you feel wonderful about yourself? Being curious, organized, or eating healthy, maybe? Enjoy finding *your* values. Just yours. You can "borrow" from someone you look up to or admire. My parents value community service, and I grew up taking meals to families who needed them. I loved doing that. It's meaningful to me. It made me feel good to see their smiling faces. I was helping my neighbor, and it also gave me a deep sense of gratitude for everything I had in my life. I felt very blessed.

High-energy Gratitude & Kick-butt Blessings

If you didn't know it, true gratitude can transform you. Honest, it can. And it relates to playing sports in every way. Because, when you think and feel deep thankfulness for the smallest things, for everything, it creates a positive mind and the highest energy. When you experience the fullness of gratitude you are grounded in goodness, life is terrific, and you will be lifted up to perform. You do not need anything else in that moment. Instead of *needing* to win and feeling nervous, which is low energy, you will be able to shift your mind and body into a sense of ease and confidence, and you'll be ready to perform from a place of peace and joy. With gratitude swimming inside you, you will not focus on what you don't have. You can focus on what you want your body to do. This frees you to do and be your best.

Practice recognizing what you have. Appreciate all you have. Make a list! Even your struggles teach you. So be thankful…

Pain? Struggle? Thanks, that's just what I wanted!

I'm lying still and stiff, in 'the white tube' —getting an MRI scan. Aw, this stinks, because one, I'm injured, and two, I'm claustrophobic. Small dark spaces elicit panic in me. But I must grit it out, because the doctor needs to diagnose my injury. It's my right knee, it's hurting again. In practice, I squatted down, it locked up, and a searing pain hit me! So it occurs to me, ugh, I can think about my knee and the pain, and feeling scared in this tight space, or…I can go somewhere else…somewhere in my imagination.

It's my junior year, fall quarter, and I compete on the gymnastics team for the University of Utah. If you didn't catch that, let me say it again—I compete. I'm not the type to give in to injury. And yet, I've been racked with many. Besides bad ankles, icing and taping every day, I had a knee surgery freshman year with a full-leg cast, then rehabbed, and surprisingly broke my back, no joke, with two months in a body-cast, sophomore year. That was miserable—my body went soft, very soft… I did a ton of rehab after that one!

In this athletic life, pain and struggle have not escaped me, and they often feel like daily companions. It's a decision to alleviate the stress; I focus on the positive option; I go into my imagination. I think of the floor music I chose for the upcoming season. I love it: "Let the music play," by Shannon. A catchy dance song on the radio, very popular. I know the music so well, every 8-count phrase, every beat, every accent. I start to imagine how I will dance to it. In fact, I begin to choreograph my own floor routine.

The MRI technician interrupts. On speaker, a flat voice says, "Lie still, we're starting the next image." I take in some air and slowly breathe out. My body, confined in the tube, reminds me to pray; I try to be calm. I close my eyes and the loud knocking sounds begin. I manage to zero in on my music. I hear it in

my mind, da…da…dada-da-da… I see moves: I pop my hip left, then right, my head whips left, then right, I snap my hand up and up…then I tumble, round-off, flip flop, double back, land… I continue this process, I hear the notes, create playful struts and steps—I dream a spectacular show piece.

Within thirty minutes I have danced in my mind and most of my floor routine is complete; a mix of jazz, hip-hop, and Broadway spunk. I like it. Finally, the MRI is over.

They slide me out of the dark machine. I look at the pale floor, white walls, everything germ-free and bare. I go back to campus. I'll hear from the doctor in the next day, they say. This is limbo…waiting.

It's miserable being injured again, not to mention shut inside an MRI tube. I don't know what will happen, how bad my knee is, if I'll get back to 100% or not. Hmm, I feel tense. I don't want to be out of the gym. But the truth is this predicament pushes me; I get out of bed every morning, lie on the carpet in my pajamas, and do two hundred crunches. I have to keep my abs strong, keep my weight down.

And because of the seriousness, I don't want to get depressed, so I go deep into my own mind and imagine great things—me performing my best. I do this to keep my hopes up, to motivate myself, to believe I can overcome anything. I pretend I'm training and hitting my routines. I'm with my teammates; we are confident and fearless. This is what I want. And I know it's the fear that provokes me to go into that other world; a healthy me in front of uniformed judges and our red Utah fans. I create my own triumph. That's the world I like. And with those positive images, I can endure and make it through another hard day.

After the MRI, the doctor schedules me for a second knee surgery (bahhh!), but it's arthroscopic, so recovery should be quicker. I have surgery, go through six weeks of agonizing rehab—many hours in the training room, sweating and climbing hills on the stationary bike, pushing and pulling weights, soaking my leg in ice water so freezing it hurts. I work with our trainer Jeff through lots of pain to gain back lost flexibility and strength. I am exhausted. Then I watch my teammates train to prepare for meet season: double twists, double pikes, Tsukaharas, release moves. Watching is hard. I'm excited for them, but I am detached and downgraded. My body is broken. I am alone. I want to work with them, yet I am bandaged up on the sidelines… Meanwhile, I go through the holidays in a weight room, the gym, the training room,

hammering myself to be ready. Gradually, I get back to basic moves on the equipment. I ice my knee and do mental training twice a day. In my mind, I practice my skills and routines as if I were competing—I feel my muscles jumping and flipping, I see myself lean and fit in a leotard, energetic in the arena, nailing my routines. But the days are endless, and the struggle stays with me. I have to push, push, push myself to get back into competition shape and feel confident once again.

Eight weeks later, it's January. I've gone through drudgery and grey clouds, and finally, light peeks through. The season begins—and I'm there. My knee is much better; I'm in good shape…and I dance. In front of the judges, my music starts bouncing, and I smile. I tumble and dance for the joy, for the crowd, and for my Utah teammates. I am full of life! And it is amazing to compete! People praise my floor routine and the judges give me solid scores. I keep icing my knee after every practice and meet, and I'm getting through as our team faces ASU, UCLA, Oregon State, and others. We are together—a whole team, an inspired team, and I continue to focus and improve.

Three and a half months later, by the end of the season, our team does the unbelievable—as underdogs, we go to Nationals and win our 5th consecutive NCAA National title. And the extra special news, I shine on floor. I am floating on air having the time of my life, and I win the NCAA National Floor title. I can't believe it. I am an NCAA National Champion!

There's no way I could've imagined that, lying in the MRI. I didn't think of winning when I was doing the rehab and feeling the pain and struggle. I simply wanted to get back in the gym and do my best. And the truth is, the injury helped me; it forced me to focus harder. I had to go inside myself and r-e-a-c-h for my inner strength. I ignored all distractions because getting healthy and competing were the most important things to me. I ate in a disciplined manner to heal quickly and to be lean and strong. I made sure I slept enough so I had energy the next day to get back on track in the gym. Every day I trained mentally, so I knew with every cell in my body that I could perform my best. Everything was done with focus, because I wanted to compete badly.

What I'm sharing is that it IS the challenge. It is the challenge that sparks us. It is the struggle that makes us want to rise! It is the pain in the journey that makes us stronger on the inside and so grateful to be able to play and compete. Sure, it's common to get hurt in sports. I know. But what is not common, is realizing that injuries can be a gift—a wonderful gift to learn about the self and grow in a way that not many experience. I am so grateful for the hurt and agony, strange as it sounds. And as a coach, I am wiser and able to relate to my athletes. Which allows them to trust me and face their hardest days, too…

64

I never wished for an injury or asked for a big challenge, but life gives it sometimes, so what are you gonna do??? Well, I say out loud: "Thanks, painful knee injury! Thank you, scary MRI! Thank you, surgery!" And of course, "Thank you, rehab! Whoopee! That's just what I wanted!"

★ ★
★ **You never know what challenges will spark deep motivation inside you. You never know what pain will turn into joy. But you can handle it. Be curious. Because life is a mystery and all you can do is trust what comes, exercise your inner strength, and enjoy the ride.**

Difficult Challenges? Say, "Thanks! That's just what I wanted!"

I condition my young athletes and push them hard. I look them in the eyes and tell them, "You will do many repetitions. Your body will hurt, your arms will cramp, and your legs will shake. You'll want to stop, but you'll keep going until your body fails. And that…that is when you are getting stronger."

These young girls, their eyes grow…and because they know what I expect and they know I am completely devoted, I add: "And guess what you'll say…?"

They grin and in unison they say: "Thanks, Coach, Lisa! That's just what I wanted!"

We all giggle.

"That's right!" I clap my hands.

When you experience that level of hard work, and you gradually see yourself getting stronger, faster, and better, then you *know* a certain kind of pain is required. And that also builds character. And wisdom. Knowing you must go through challenges in order to rise, this creates such a strength inside yourself. You are stronger than you think you are…

This. Is. *Good.*

Injured?

It's the same for injuries. When you get injured, know that your body heals. I'll say it again, learn that your body heals. Learn to assist the healing process. Doctors and physical therapists recommend rest, ice, compression, elevation (R.I.C.E.). You may also take Aspirin for pain, or for pain & swelling, Ibuprofen is an over-the-counter anti-inflammatory. Be active in rehab and recovery. Don't wait. Help the healing! You will be a stronger athlete for managing this wisely and positively. Say this: I will be better for managing my injuries well.

Do you understand? You will be stronger. You will.

Thanks! That's just what I wanted!

Lost a Game?

No one likes to lose, but everyone does. Everyone does. Even the best athletes lose, sometimes. When you lose a race, a competition or match, choose to learn from it. Learn what it takes to do better next time.

Decide to use mental skills:

1.   Take a deep breath
2.   Speak positively to yourself
3.   Visualize what you want to create

Some athletes are motivated by failure. I totally get that. After a loss, they are more motivated to work harder and win the next time. They've got grit and fight.

But if you stay bummed out, I understand that, too. Sit with it for a while, because it's real and your emotions are important. Then, after the initial sinking feeling of losing, think about what you really want and choose to rebound.

Decide: "I'll be okay. I am resilient and I will try again."

Start to visualize and imagine yourself better next time. Congratulate the winner and move on to a new approach for tomorrow's game. A Loss is a teacher. It is. It teaches us to be resilient, to grow and try something different. Losing pushes us to think of new strategies. So be thankful for the push! Thankful for the loss.

Injured? Okay. Say, "Thank you, I'll get better."

Failure? Okay. Say, "Thank you, I am learning."

Think, *It's okay. I can take it. And watch. . . I'll make something good happen next.*

If I am to Fail

If, today, I fail,
my chin will sink low,
my shoulders,
slump forward,
my sigh will go on;
but only for a minute.

So dare me,
I'm not afraid,
I'm sick,
sick and tired of my own
doubt,
my own fear
of never being what I hope,
or what I want.

Oh come on, dare me.
I dare myself,
and tomorrow, the sun will rise,
and my chin, even higher,
my shoulders,
cocksure.
And it'll be you
who feels the fear,

because I am strong.
I won't fail.
As a matter of fact,
I'll wear a smile,
and tomorrow,
I'll kick your ass.

Kick-butt Practices and Exercises for Chapter 4

Exercise: Know Yourself

What do you like or dislike about yourself? What things interest you? Write in your notebook what changes you want to make in the world. Because you are powerful. You are. Also write your strengths and talents. Then, the areas you want to improve. This is your own character profile. It's about You. Read it and reflect on the person you are, today, and how you will keep evolving, keep getting better.

Exercise: "I'm Terrific!"

I dare you. Stand in front of your mirror every day for 10 seconds, 30 days in a row…say, "I'm Terrific!" and believe it. (And write it in your notebook.) This literally impacts your thinking. To the guys who are reading this…I double-dog dare you.

Exercise: Identify Your Core Values

1. Choose your Top 10 Values from this list and write them down. Not your parents' values. Not your friend's values. Not even your coach's values. Unless you 100% agree. But be sure to choose *yours*. It may be challenging! There are many good ones! But go slowly and consider what is most important to you.

Core Values

Family	Teamwork	Caring
Trust	Winning	Open-minded
Safety	Integrity	Acceptance
Clear Communication	Gratitude	Committed
Patience	Discipline	Health, mental &
Curiosity	Hard work	physical
Learning	Equality	Passion
Kindness	Spirituality	Courage
Relationships	Fun	Global affairs
Respect	Balance	Innovative
Adventure	Impact	Excellence
Resilience	Success	Optimistic
Humility	Leadership	
Achievement	Creativity	

2. Now, look at the top 10 you chose, look closely… Can you narrow the list to your top 5?

One of my clients, a Division I college soccer player, chose this list as her top 5: Integrity, Learning, Discipline, Impact, Passion. This exercise helped her to be closely in tune with herself. She better understood what is most important to her, and she decided to not get sucked into what other people think and say. She wants to be stronger in her own mind and choices. This exercise made her feel really great!

3. Finally, put your top 5 in order: 1st, 2nd, 3rd, etc. Really dig deep and decide.

Be aware, this is what you think, today. You may choose differently in 3-6 months as you go through life experiences. Which is totally normal and good. You are evolving!

4. Use this list of Values to stay connected to yourself. To feel good about being a person of virtue—working and practicing to be your best self. Your highest self. Because staying connected to your core values allows you to feel strong inside. And that will only help you achieve your goals.

5. Feel free to do this exercise with someone else you want to get to know better. Someone you'd like to talk to and share your values. This is a wonderful way to connect with family, friends, teammates, etc. And it makes you feel great.

Exercise: Write and Say "Thank You"

Fill self with High-energy Gratitude. Say, "Thank you" each morning. Say, "Thank you" to someone…or no one. It's up to you. Say, "Thank you" to the universe, to God, to the sky, to your dog—you decide. Use a calm voice. Take a breath and exhale before each line…and feel free to say it quietly.

Say: "Thank you"

Say: "Thank you for everything I have."

Say: "Thank you for the clothes I wear. Thank you for the shoes on my feet. Thank you for the bed I sleep in. Thank you for the food I eat."

Say: "Thank you."

Feel it. Feel the gratitude, for there are many in the world who do not have even the basic needs.

You play sports…

Say: "Thank you. Thank you for this opportunity to play. Thank you for the field. Thank you for my teammates. Thank you for my coaches," etc.

Feel the gratitude.

Exercise: Write a 'Thank You' Script or a Prayer of Thanks

From the above Gratitude Exercise, now, write your own 'thank you' script. When you write your own thoughts and words, it will be more powerful in changing or creating what you want. Make it meaningful for you. Write your 'Thank You' script now…and use this daily. And before bed is a good time to read it and say thank you. Positive thoughts before sleep help you feel peaceful and may even give you good dreams!

70

Chapter 5

Fears: Notice, Manage, Conquer

Fear *hits* you.

It seems to come out of nowhere. But fear often comes from something that happened in the past. Or, what might happen in the future. Fear emerges…and it stops you. When a scary thought or feeling shows up, it's normal to hold back. Athletes, however, aren't supposed to hesitate or be uncertain. They need to perform, play, and compete! So what can athletes do when they feel afraid?

Can't Go On

Kiera didn't like the intense pain of running the 800 fast. In fact, she dreaded it. She was terribly afraid. "All I can think is, I don't want to do this, it's going to hurt so bad. I just want to go home," she told me in a mental training session. It was her sophomore year on the track team in high school, and even though Kiera was determined to make fast enough times to run in college, she shrank from giving a full effort. She did not attack. No matter how much she wanted to do well, she couldn't overcome her fear. In all the world, humans experience pain, athletes in particular. So how do you manage?

I asked Kiera, "Have you ever heard the phrase, Welcome the pain, or Embrace the pain?" She hadn't.

I described the point of exhaustion, when athletes hurt and feel they can't go on, the pain is so powerful it can convince you to weaken or give up. I told Kiera that when you know and believe that experiencing that type of pain is good and will only make you better, then you want it. Because that intense fatigue means you are reaching your goal.

I told her a story when I was training for Elite and conditioning super hard. My coach pushed and yelled while my teammates and I did hundreds and hundreds of repetitions—sit ups, push-ups, lunges, and squat jumps—it was endless. My body shook and cramped. We couldn't stop or he'd give us more, and yet the pain was excruciating. Some of my teammates couldn't take it, they stopped and cried. Then we were told to do more. Clearly, we were learning to be tough but some couldn't handle it.

I told myself the physical suffering was good for me. I knew I would get stronger and better because of it. I decided…the pain is good. In the midst of it, I said to myself, "One more, one more, one more, keep going, keep going, keep going…" and somehow, I got through it. I didn't want to stop because as much as it hurt, and boy did it hurt, I wanted to get stronger more than I wanted to stop. Kiera listened and understood. As she sat on the couch, her body relaxed and her face softened. I could practically see her thoughts changing: pain is agonizing, but maybe, maybe she could manage it and run faster. I guided her to close her eyes and visualize her upcoming race. I prompted her to breathe and relax, imagine the track and the other runners around her. I told her to run the way she wanted to run, fast, not holding back. She will feel the pain, but she will breathe, focus on her arms, her stride, and run through the pain to the finish line. "See" yourself run the entire race, the agony will come, but you can keep going and you will use your positive script to help you. In a previous session, Kiera had created a script with phrases that would boost her confidence: I am strong, I am fast, I will finish. She would say these words to herself before the race, and during the race when it hurts.

She sat, closed her eyes, and visualized. It only took a couple minutes. Afterwards, Kiera reported it was helpful. She was learning a new approach to handle the pain and still run fast. I instructed her to practice this vision of embracing the pain—running her race feeling it, knowing she's getting stronger and faster. She would repeat her script and make it to the finish line. She agreed to keep practicing this mental image.

We ended the session with a concrete reminder: a sign. I told her she needs to remind herself she can do this, that she can embrace the pain. I gave her paper and markers and offered her ideas of what she could write. Kiera thought… then she focused and leaned over the coffee table. She created a sign to post in her room.

She wrote: "The pain makes me better!" She looked at me… and smiled.

Managing pain and fear is not easy. It takes real intention to learn and apply the mental tools, and then practice. Kiera made great improvements in her subsequent races. Her confidence grew and she reached her goal to run in college.

Mindset: Impermanence

Impermanence is the understanding that everything in existence is temporary and transient. Things change and pass, lives constantly fluctuate and evolve. Nothing is permanent or forever enduring. Do not get a cloudy mind over a mistake, loss, pain, or injury. It will be difficult, but it passes. Sadness passes. Fear passes. Newness always comes.

Fear is Temporary

It comes and goes to and from your mind, and from person to person. It passes. When you feel afraid, *don't* give up. Though great fear seems unbearable at times, you can master your thoughts to deal with it. Tense scary moments are simply a challenge. You can look at the facts, choose a strategy, and go in a new direction. You can take steps and overcome and you *can* be successful.

After my terrible, freaky crash on my head in gymnastics at age 15, I had the worst fear of my life! I froze up. My coaches yelled. I panicked... For weeks, I cried. And I lost nearly all of my skills. I regressed into the insecure mind of a beginner and I was going to quit. I felt like nothing. Until a sport psychologist helped me to understand what mental skills were and how to use them. I trained and trained, hours, weeks, and months. I re-learned gymnastics in slow motion, like an infant...rolling over, sitting up, crawling, walking—it took time. But gradually, I managed my thoughts; I focused on my body positions, and overcame the fear. Months later, at the USA Junior Olympics, I won two national championship titles. That long struggle was both the hardest and most thrilling journey of my life. And if I could do it, I believe you can, too. Don't give up.

You are Not Your Mistake

Athletes are supposed to be strong and almighty like Superman or Wonder Woman! You run and sweat, reach for goals, deal with injuries, compete under pressure, push yourself to become better and better, and yet…you can be very negative. You cut yourself down and self-criticize when you make mistakes, maybe even when you don't make a mistake. You're just hard on yourself.

I get it. Athletes want to feel and be successful, but they often keep track and measure themselves by their faults. If you have a great day in practice, you're good. If you mess up a lot, you are terrible.

I would like to clarify this perspective: You are not the sum of your mistakes, nor do they make you terrible. You are a fabulous and unique you, striving and pursuing your dreams. Mistakes are part of the process of learning and becoming great.

MISTAKES, ACCIDENTS, AND INJURIES ARE GOOD TEACHERS

I even tell my clients, "Yes, you are *becoming*, but you're also great right now!" The most celebrated athletes have miscalculated, fallen, and made many errors. And that made them better. The fact is when you take risks and see your errors as *coursework*, your failures and setbacks are a way to spark you to change. You realize it's all part of the journey. Struggles and mistakes are *vital* to learning. *Accept whatever happens.*

If you stay in a "safe zone" to avoid a stumble, then you're playing it safe. Holding back. And you're likely afraid that you'll look bad or be embarrassed…so you are careful. Well, in sports, careful does not a champion make. You need to be aggressive and take risks. I dare you, after your next flub-up, say: "I'm learning and I'm great!"

Become Wiser

The truth about mistakes, accidents, and injuries is that you really can learn best from them. As human beings, we don't like to mess up—but we remember. And then we can correct ourselves. After your next error, choose whether you want to feel defeated, or if you want to rise. I suggest you readjust. Refocus on a new strategy. Get sharper, learn, shine from the inside—rise. Feel good that you're facing challenges, making improvements, and growing in understanding. If you're on a team, you are shaping a positive team attitude. You can also empathize with others when they are struggling. You can help teammates improve from *your mistakes* and failures. The athlete in you is not only tough, but intelligent and courageous. In facing the fear of failure, you are stronger. And wiser.

Shattered

When Doug was 11 years old in Little League, there was an incident. A scary and painful one. During a baseball game, Doug was at bat facing a talented pitcher. A wild fast pitch flew toward the plate. Doug reacted, put his arm out, and the ball bashed his elbow; it shattered.

He went through severe pain, embarrassment, surgery, and rehab. He regretted putting his arm up, but he knew he'd never do that again.

Now, at age 16, the memory of the accident and the pain gives Doug anxiety. He feels very hesitant at bat. Whenever he faces a fast pitch, he does not step *toward* the pitcher when he swings. He doubts his abilities and fears he'll get hit by the ball.

I told Doug, "Let's take a close look at your eleven-year-old self." We talked. I learned that when he was eleven and in 5th grade, he had never faced a fast, wild pitch. His coach did not prepare him or tell him how to move when a wild pitch comes. He had slow reaction time. The pitcher in that game was unusually fast for his age group. All of these facts had contributed to his poor response. It became clear that he was not able to handle the situation well.

Then we began to assess him at his current age. I found out that Doug is a sophomore in high school. He plays at a high level of baseball. He has many years of experience, excellent training with good coaches, and he's played in many games. He understands how to move and answer a wild pitch now. He has quick reaction time. Fast pitchers are more common for his age group. And, Doug's intentions are to someday play in the big leagues.

He was starting to see the difference. When he was young, he was inexperienced and unprepared. Now, Doug is knowledgeable, fast, and very skilled!

We did an exercise to help him practice a sharper focus on himself: *What CAN you control on your path to achieving your goals.* This reminded Doug that he *cannot* control the pitch or the pitcher. He can only control himself, how he watches the ball, how he is in tune with his breath and physical readiness, how he moves and responds to each pitch. And I emphasized how he needs to

IN THE ZONE . . .

concentrate on his own power, directing his body position and technique while facing a fast pitcher. He has power.

Doug confirmed that he liked reading and thinking about his current 16-year-old self. It felt good to recognize his strengths. The funny-bone injury was scary and painful. But he admitted that he had learned a lot from that experience. I reiterated that he is on track to the big leagues. The past fear has affected him, but if he thinks about it now, his eleven-year-old self was a teacher for him; he learned.

I suggested to Doug that he address his 11-year-old self and say 'thank you, thank you for teaching me.' So he did it. Doug recognized that since that painful experience, he was now very grateful. His pain and fear were teachers, too.

We ended our discussion with Doug visualizing himself at bat, being more in tune with his abilities, more confident in his body. He imagined a fast pitch coming at him and stepping toward the pitcher while swinging. He saw it. And he felt better. **Then Doug created a script: I want to step toward the pitcher at bat. I will step toward the pitcher at bat. I step toward the pitcher at bat. Doug is now in control.**

Let's Break it Down

When Doug's accident happened and fear took over, he didn't work through it or get a new perspective. Instead, he stuffed down the fear and carried it for five years. Fear controlled him until 1) he talked about it, 2) understood it, and 3) connected to his current knowledge and abilities. This process was pivotal. Most athletes try to hide their fear, they walk around, play sports trying to be tough, hoping it'll go away. But when you hold fear inside, it will stay with you and torment you. A better plan is to pause…understand your fear, diffuse it, and take charge.

Conquer Fear—Take Steps to Diffuse It

When a person is going to face a big challenge, tension and anxiety show up.

Athletes, please don't stress. Nerves and fear are normal. If you think you're weird for feeling so nervous, you're not. It's normal. And you will be fine. Put your attention on yourself. Notice the signs of nerves and fear creeping up on you: your hair stands up, your stomach turns, your thoughts race, you worry about everything, you sweat. Get curious and understand the fear, exactly where and when it starts and why. Are you nervous someone will think you look bad? Are you afraid someone will criticize you? Are you worried you will fail?

Recognize these are in the future and outside of your control. The reality of the situation is that you can only control *yourself*…in the *present moment*.

Instead of pushing down or ignoring the nervousness, pause for a moment, and embrace the present reality, not what might happen, but what's happening now. Shift your attention to a next step, take a breath, or even slow down and do a basic step or skill in your sport. Focusing your mind and body on performing a basic move can ease your tension and connect you to what you're

good at. What's easy. Most importantly, breathe, breathe, breathe—*deeply*—and focus on what you *can control*. Get back in charge of your thoughts and emotions. When you feel out of control and try to ignore the fear, it will keep coming up again, and again, and tighten you up.

Types of Fear

Athletes experience many fears. Some of them are:

1. Fear of tension / a stressful conversation

2. Fear of criticism / not being good enough

3. Fear of pain / getting injured or hurt

4. Fear of rejection by a coach or teammates

5. Fear of failure / not reaching your goal

6. Fear of not being an athlete / losing your identity

7. Fear of being in the wrong sport / not the right abilities or body type

8. Fear of being judged that you have no value / you're nothing

The truth is these are scary thoughts, they are not hungry lions about to eat you, these are thoughts. You can overcome these fearful thoughts with mental skills and targeted mindsets. It takes awareness and practice. Your positive thoughts and energy will change how you see the world. Your thoughts and energy will also change how others see you! Meanwhile, notice your thought patterns…

Just Notice

If a thought comes to your mind, like I'm scared, just notice it. Notice you are beginning to feel scared. Like Ben, my golf client: he'd prepare to hit the ball, but got nervous because other players were watching him. He was scared to blow it or look bad. Fear made him tense up and he ended up doing exactly what he was afraid to do—he hit a bad shot. Every athlete needs to ask themselves, do I want to keep thinking this thought? How does it make me feel, and what am I doing? If you feel tentative, like you won't be aggressive, then decide to change your thoughts.

Emotions can overwhelm you—that's understandable—and then confusion or panic develops, and it's hard to make a good choice. You're overwhelmed! The trick in 'noticing' is to catch the fear in the beginning, just as it's starting. Then you can think more clearly. And while observing your mind, "Uh oh, a scary thought." When recognized, you can decide to change your mental pattern. Redirect your mind.

Plan to Re-direct your Mind

Before practice or a game, make a plan ahead of time to be in tune with yourself. For instance: "I will pay attention to my thoughts. I will focus on myself. I will take a breath when I feel tense." This is key to being mentally in control. And when you want to switch from fear to optimism, ask yourself, "What do I want to focus on next?" Breathing is a terrific start! To shift into positive thoughts and action, it starts with a breath—inhale and exhale all the way. Consider doing an easier move or skill that gives you confidence. When you're ready to tackle the challenge that caused your anxiety, break it down into parts. Go slowly. Even if it's *just* in your mind. But physically doing parts can help a lot! Simple steps. First, awareness…take a deep breath…then desire… then action.

Exactly What is Your Fear?

To be able to let go of fear and move on, it helps to understand exactly what is making you anxious. Every athlete and sport is different, but the experiences that cause fear are similar. For example: striking out at bat, missing a soccer goal or tennis shot and losing, looking unskilled or like you don't belong, a coach getting frustrated and ignoring you, falling on your head and getting hurt on a back flip, or letting down your parents after they've spent so much time and money on you.

Do you know what is worrying you? What makes you nervous? Just remember, if it's something from the past or a hypothetical future, you can't control it. The trick is to get calm and focus on the present moment. Then take steps to create what you want.

What to Focus on When Worries or Fears Begin: the Key is to *Slow Down.*

Consider the Baseball Player at bat...

Approaching the batter's box, he needs to connect to the present moment—not the past, not the future...the now. In uniform, helmet on, bat in hands, pitcher on the mound. Feel the sun or cool air. Baseball player suddenly worries, thinks about past 'at bats' when he failed and struck out. He's afraid he isn't good enough, he'll fail *again*... He lacks confidence.

Slow down, focus on present moment.

· Look inside yourself, not at everyone else, zoom into yourself.

· Let go of future, possible mistakes. Think of now.

· Say your positive script or thoughts: "I am confident. I can do this."

· Check your position/feet/arms/ technique.

· Think of your body feeling agile, quick, strong.

· Stop and breathe deeply, is it flowing?

· Take a few deep breaths, exhale all the way.

· Get calm and loose by releasing tightness in the body.

· Think of your intention to be ready for the ball: "I'm ready."

· Know you've hit the ball before, and you will hit it again. "I hit the ball."

· Say, "I swing. I make contact," or something that feels confident.

· Click into determination and trust: "I trust my abilities and my training. I can do this!"

In the Trenches with Paralyzing Fear

As a coach, I work closely with my athletes and they trust me. One of my young gymnasts triumphed after experiencing awful fear. We worked together for a few months and it was not easy; she went back and forth. She would make an improvement and feel great, high fives and smiles. Then in a split second, she regressed. The fear seemed to come out of nowhere and she froze up. It was terrible.

Paralyzed

Maria, Mental Skills Training #4

Learning mental skills in the upstairs room, Maria and I sat at the table and talked about the last week. We looked at her notebook and reviewed the tools she's been using and how often. She is 10 years old and understands that mental practice is very important. At this stage of the season, she's behind her teammates. She's been afraid to do the same skills they're practicing, and the coach has helped as much as she can. But Maria is stressed. She wants to keep moving forward, but she is scared. She loves gymnastics and wants to advance.

And then she decided, "I want to do a back tuck in the gym." We reviewed her script for the standing back tuck. We practiced deep breathing and visualizing the skill in parts and being successful. This went well. Maria takes it seriously and goes through each part with me. She reports that she can "see" the skill in her mind, but can't always "feel" it in her body. This is normal, since she is just beginning to learn these tools.

MENTAL SCRIPT—BACK HANDSPRING

PREPARE   SWING DOWN   JUMP BACK   REACH

Downstairs to the floor in the gym… Applying mental skills to the back tuck in the gym was next. Maria stretched and warmed up, then we got into basic power skills: round-offs, back handsprings, etc. For a back tuck, she needs power. And performing basics well gives her confidence. Before facing a challenge, an athlete needs to feel confident about their abilities and be in tune with their body.

We pulled a panel mat over and put it on the floor. It's about 16 inches high. I also got a sting mat, a 1.5 inch soft mat, and placed it behind the panel mat for landing. I was pretty sure Maria could do the back tuck with me spotting her. And she wanted to. But she immediately "hit the fear wall" and could not do the back tuck with a spot. She was very afraid and got quiet. I asked if there was another location, a safer place, she felt she could do the back tuck. We went to the resi pit and brought the panel mat. This is a much softer landing area.

We did several progressions—she did a simple stretch jump while I spotted her. Then, lying down on the floor on her back, she snapped her legs from a long 'straight' position into a tuck position. We reviewed her mental script, she visualized the skill, but she still could not do the back tuck. I had her lean back into my arms and I literally carried her through the move in slow motion. She is light, and I easily held her and turned her body through the back-tuck position. We did these multiple times for her to remember the *feeling of flipping upside down and turning over onto her feet.* Eventually, Maria felt better. She started to jump a little. With my hands holding her, she exerted a small jump and I carried her through the rest of the flip. We did that four times. She grew more familiar with the sequence of movement. Then she jumped much higher and did it super well.

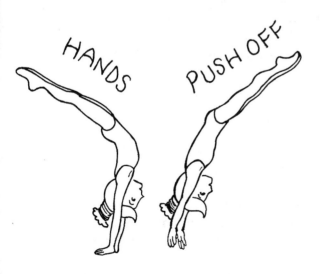

In between turns she reviewed a pattern. She applied mental skills *before* the back tuck: Breathe—Focus on her script—Action. I counted for her "1, 2, 3 jump!" Maria trusted me. She made great progress in a few minutes. But then, in a split second, she hit the fear wall again.

She regressed and became very scared. She could not do the back tuck at all. Maria freaked out: how can this happen? What's wrong with me? I just did a number of back tucks, and now I can't!

Tears welled up in her eyes. She was confused, scared, and overwhelmed.

I spoke to her gently, and we started over again. We simplified the back tuck into parts. Again, she did the drills, and I carried her through the move. Slowly, slowly, she worked back up to a mid-level where she was doing a small jump and going for it about 70% with my help. Fortunately, she was able to trust me and work with me. Maria learned that she could overcome the fear with mental skills and with my help. I was very pleased. She was brave and also happy.

My Analysis: Working through that terrible, fearful place in learning the back tuck was revealing. Maria has all the talent—she can jump and flip just fine! But her fear is extremely high. I also noticed that she 'loses the feeling' of how to do the back tuck. Fear does that. It causes the brain to "go blank" or "forget."

It was not likely that Maria would overcome this intense fear in just two more sessions. I would've been thrilled if she did. But for this level of fear, she needed the most patience from all involved, me, her parents, her coaches. Having worked with athletes with intense fears, I knew it could take 6-10 sessions, easily. We would have to see.

Continuing the exercises paid off. Maria learned and practiced the mental skills with me; she applied them, gradually, and with time, she learned to manage her fear. Maria was a Level 4 gymnast at that time, trying to move up to Level 5. She is doing great, now. She moved up and she's learned many advanced gymnastics skills. And continues to be determined! I am lucky to have worked with Maria, because she is very brave to face her fears, and she continues to use the mental skills.

Facing Fear Means Slowing Down

Like Maria, when paralyzing fear shows up, you need to go through a step-by-step process and expect setbacks. Guiding an athlete through these over-whelming emotions requires insight, mental tools, and incredible patience from a mental skills coach. Whether an athlete is struggling with a minor or extreme fear, developing mental skills to overcome it is an important aspect of successful training. When you experience fear, find a sport psychologist or a mental skills coach, who knows how to work with athletes who struggle with fear. He/She will guide you in learning and practicing the tools to get back on a confident track—and triumph!

★ Kick-butt Practices and Exercises for Chapter 5 ★

Traffic Signal—Become Aware of Fear Levels

Catch it sooner! Understand how fear builds from small to big to being totally frozen. Learn to control it using the model of a traffic signal. When you are playing or competing:

a.   Green Light—No fear, optimistic, focused, full action, move forward!

b.   Yellow Light—Nerves, doubts, fear starts, focus is interrupted, action is tense/not controlled, slow down, breathe, readjust.

c.   Red Light—Stop! Stop!! Stop!!! Highest fear! Can't focus at all, body shuts down, cannot perform. Step aside, breathe deeply, and apply mental skills. Maybe take a break.

STOP! STOP! FEAR!
CAN'T FOCUS. BODY FREEZES.

SLOW DOWN. ANXIOUS.
DOUBTING YOURSELF.

OPTIMISTIC. CONFIDENT.
FOCUSED! GO! GO! GO!

As you become more aware of these three levels, green, yellow, and red light, and observe yourself, you can pause and decide on a new strategy. Don't keep going and intensify the fear. Slow down, readjust, refocus.

Become aware: What is a green-light moment for you? Think and recall that feeling.

Describe: What is a yellow light moment when you need to slow down and readjust?

Write: Briefly describe a red-light experience, when you froze up completely.

Awareness of the levels will help you know when to pause or readjust. If you create a strategy in advance and practice in advance, you will be prepared to manage a difficult moment.

I learned this Traffic Signal model when I was a teenager, while working with Dr. Ken Ravizza at Cal-State Fullerton. I had acute fear, the worst, and I would completely shut down. He really helped me to understand myself, my mind, and how fear starts and grows. I learned how to assign a yellow or red light when I tightened up. I knew what green 'felt' like. And I figured out how to go back to green by slowing down, doing simple positions and moves I could easily perform, and felt confident doing. I learned to control my thoughts and let the fear pass.

Exercise: Become Aware of the Signs of Fear…

What signs do you experience? When does it occur? Circle the ones you know and keep noticing. Understand your body's reaction to fearful thoughts.

·1 muscles tense up

·2 stomach aches badly/butterflies

·3 hair on arms and neck stand up

·4 goosebumps/chills

·5 sweaty hands/feet

·6 mind is confused, worried, panicky

·7 sudden images of worst possible scenario

·8 emotions feel overwhelming, tears come, not able to talk or perform

Now, take steps to slow down… .

Exercise: Slow Down

Learning to slow down helps you manage your thoughts and fears.

How to do it: Write your own "at bat" script for you and your sport. When you are about to kick, hit, or do a tough move or play, use a script. Create steps and words you say to yourself to be positive and focused in the present moment. For example:

Take a breath.
I am relaxed.
I am in position.
I can do this.

Practice your script. Say it out loud during practice, days before a game or race. Imagine being in the game moment and how you want to feel confident.

Repeat your script and breathe. You will be focused in the moment. You will be focused on yourself and not worried about potential failure.

Remember: *Only you* control your body. You can't control the pitcher on the mound, or the pitch, or the officials or judges, the scores, or your coach. If you're worried about other people, then you are distracted from your body. You only control *how you respond*. For a baseball player, you control your grip on the bat, your breath, and how you swing. But you can't control the pitcher, the game, the sun or the clouds. Only you.

Past or future thoughts, no good: Almost all fears are about something in the *past* or something in the *future*. What happened a minute ago, in the last play, how you missed. Or you think about last year when you got injured, how much it hurt and how you couldn't play for a while. You are producing fear with your thoughts—you hold onto the fear of failure or getting hurt. You are attached to negativity. *Notice what you're thinking.* Your thoughts and worries spiral in your head. The fear escalates till it's extremely stressful! You need to detach from results and from other people. Slow down. Use a script. And cut the cord.

Exercise: Cut the Cord

Fear can feel like a monster—it scares you, attacks you with pressure, doubt, and confusion.

A couple athletes I coached experienced that sudden fear. They were shaken. Certainly not able to perform or play well. A 14-year-old gymnast was frequently yelled at and pressured by her coach. And a 15-year-old baseball player was scared to face a hard-throwing pitcher. The fear was immediate. In their minds, they created a mental barrier for success. He tensed up at bat, she froze at the chalk box. They both let the "fear monster" paralyze them.

These athletes allowed the coach and the pitcher to control their thoughts and emotions, so I taught them how to disconnect.

How to do it:

1. Imagine a pair of scissors. Do you see them? Now imagine a cord, like a rubber cord, attached to you and the coach/person who is affecting you, causing you to feel nervous. You two are attached!

2. Imagine you have the scissors in your hand. Reach the scissors toward the cord that is connecting you two and *cut it! Cut the cord!* Hear and *see* it "snip!" and feel disconnected. Imagine you are separate and cannot feel their tension any longer.

3. Now, you just observe the other person (coach or whoever). Just watch and listen, and think your own thoughts. Be respectful, and simply focus on what you want.

Exercise: Talk to Self and Shift Out of Fear

The trick is to become aware when fear is just starting to creep up on you.

So first, be aware.

How to do it: When you begin to feel afraid and experience the symptoms of fear, then decide to shift with these steps:

1. "I notice I'm feeling scared." Acknowledge to yourself the fact that fear is starting—you are feeling very uncomfortable.

2. "Okay…it's okay." Saying, 'okay' is more than acknowledging you're aware—you're keeping cool because there's no need to panic. Nothing's *wrong* with you; it's *normal* to feel afraid. Everyone experiences fear. It's normal.

3. "Pause…I will let go of the outcome." You are not perfect, forget the score, let go of the coach's expectation. You are distracted. Your mind is somewhere else. Come back to the present moment in the details of your breath and body.

4. "I can slow down…I can take a step back…" Shift thoughts to alternative action; you can repeat an earlier progression or easier skill to get your mind back in the groove of knowing and feeling confident.

5. "I can take deep breaths and connect with my body." Calm yourself with deep breathing, refocus mind to feeling calm or energetic, quick, strong.

6. "I can visualize." Recall/Visualize yourself performing a skill correctly and successfully, several times. See yourself doing well.

7. "I can repeat my best technique and a mental script in my mind." Talk to yourself like a positive coach and guide your body in basic steps. Use cue words, like 'jump, extend, reach…'

8. "I can get reassurance from a coach or teammate to be present and confident in my ability." When you get someone's positive energy, it can comfort and encourage you, and rebuild your confidence.

Trust

Finally, trust your training, trust your abilities. Your body is smart. I'll say it again—your body is smart. Sometimes, we think too much! We second guess and doubt and our thoughts spin into worry and possible failure. Oh no! What do I do? And we freak out.

After I completed my mental training with Dr. Ravizza and I got back into competition, I was still scared at times. I'd even be in a competition, my floor music was playing, judges watching, and I'd forget how to do my tumbling pass (a double full). My mind went blank! But the music was playing, so what could I do? Either walk off the floor and quit. *Or trust.*

I tossed up a Hail Mary and trusted my body—I ran and started to tumble, and guess what, my body did the double full and I landed on my feet. Safely. I was amazed I did it!

Accept

The best remedy for fear is accepting it. It happens. But it doesn't have to rule you. Fear is part of sports, part of being human, and training mentally is the key to managing it. These strategies in Chapter 5 are extremely helpful. But in order to avoid ongoing and recurring fears, or to conquer the most terrible fears, you will need to pursue a mental skills coach or sport psychologist and do the work. Train mentally. Practice awareness of your thoughts, get in tune with your body (tense or relaxed), practice calming & relaxing techniques regularly, repeat positive statements, rehearse written scripts for your skills, and visualize successful actions and movements. You can handle it. *You can overcome.*

Chapter 6

Manifest Success and Self-Belief

What do you want?

And what do you believe?

My Left Side

On our NJB basketball team, Taylor was thirteen. She shot best with her right hand. She was right-handed. I was coaching, and the team was doing a drill: right side lay-ups. Taylor did great. Her ponytail swished side to side as she made seven out of ten shots on her right side. Then we switched over to the left side of the basket. Everyone lined up, and one-by-one, the girls dribbled the ball to the hoop, going up for a shot with their left hand.

Taylor was not a naturally-talented athlete and struggled. Each turn, she kept missing her left side, and each time she missed, she became more frustrated. I watched her in between turns, her body slouched, eyes on the floor. After six misses in a row, and the other girls were hitting their shots, I said, "Taylor, come here."

She immediately frowned and blurted out, "I can't make my left side!" Hm. Yeah, all the missed shots were proof for her, and clearly, she believed it. She believed that she could not make it.

I paused and looked her right in the eye: "You *can't*…?"

She nodded, "I can't make it."

So I gently put my hand on her shoulder. "Well, do you know that if you say you can't…then you can't… You've already decided."

Taylor's eyes opened wide. This was curious.

Then I asked, "Do you *want* to make your left side?"

"Yes!" she snapped. "I want to make it." And she did. I could feel it.

"Okay." And I looked at her more seriously. "Then you need to say, 'I can do it!'" And imagine your left hand reaching and putting the ball through the hoop. Can you close your eyes and imagine it?"

She did it. Right there, she stood with me and closed her eyes for a few seconds. Then she opened them and looked at me.

"What are you going to say?" I asked.

"I can do it," she replied.

"Yes. You can." I looked at her with complete sureness, because I knew she could do it. Beneath her frustration was great desire.

Taylor took a breath and went back to the line with a strong walk. When it was her turn, she held the ball and I stepped in front of the hoop like a defender. She came toward me, dribbling to the basket with a fierce look on her face. I held my hands up and yelled, "You can do it, you can do it, you can do it!" And right over my head, she jumped, reached her left hand upward, and tossed the ball right through the net.

Wow! Fantastic! Made it on her first try! She smiled. We high fived, and she got right back in line. From across the court, I called to her to repeat, "I can do it" three times, and to see her hand putting the ball through the hoop. "Take a breath and focus!" I urged. She nodded, okay.

The team kept doing lay ups, and then it was Taylor's turn again. She took a breath and began. I stood in front of the hoop and called, "You can do it!" Her eyes zoomed in on the hoop, and sure enough, she made it again! Wow!

Taylor didn't flinch. She got back in line, taller and more energetic than anyone on the court. The momentum of hitting two shots in a row seemed to drive her. It's like she was now saying to herself, "I *make* my left side, I *make* my left side." Her third turn came up, she took a breath again, and focused. She dribbled toward me, focused on the ball, then she jumped… She made her left-side *again*! Three times in a row!

I was so happy, and then I realized it's not a huge surprise. I knew she changed her thoughts and she believed in the possibility. She really did manifest the three baskets with her mind. I watched the whole thing. But what blew me away is how determined she was, how focused she was, and that she accomplished it 1, 2, 3, so quickly.

The entire team saw what Taylor did, and that kind of energy and determination was contagious.

That day, Taylor grew more confident in herself, and her attitude and performance pushed her teammates to play their best. By the end of that season, we were Division Champs.

Taylor didn't realize what she started, that believing truly helped us win.

The Skill of Believing

Believing is a learned skill and it begins with a desire. And I don't mean believing in a fantasy, like having super powers, although you can pretend. What I mean is believing in something real that you're preparing for. Something that is in the context of your life. When you connect to your desire, you will also feel charged up. As you face challenges in making a shot or a move, or playing your best game, you can choose to get in tune with your desire and believe that it will happen…or it won't. If you *believe it will*, then you're more likely to achieve.

Taylor had the desire to make her left-handed lay-up. She was open to my suggestion to say and imagine a successful shot. And then, she did not think of her missed shots when she was saying, "I can do it!" She focused on the vision of making it. So you need to let go of previous errors and failures and concentrate on the upcoming success. Then keep your mind in the present moment: the run, the dribble, your hand, the ball, aiming for the target, etc.

Within a practice session, in a few moments, you can shift from frustration to manifesting success. And it will affect your whole season. Believe it.

Weeding

My mother sang. She sang in the church choir, she sang in the kitchen while cooking, she sang to her babies, and…she sang with me in the yard while we pulled weeds.

There were times it was just me and my mom. All my brothers and sisters did yard work, too—we took turns and mowed the lawn, raked leaves, and pulled weeds on a Saturday. We even cleaned out the garage and swept it.

But on special occasions, my mom said she and I would go out and weed together. We'd make an offering, a sacrifice of work for God. I learned this was like a prayer in action. Hm, I was twelve years old, I believed in prayer, so I followed along, though I wasn't excited about it. *Weeding.*

But then she made it fun. Because that's my mom, she's fun. She asked what my goal was for my next competition, because she often asked me that, and I told her: "I want to score a 9."

And she said, "Great!"

In gymnastics, a 10.0 is perfect, as you may know. And I had scored in the high eights, but never a nine. I wanted it so badly.

We sat on the sidewalk digging in the dirt with garden tools. My mom decided to make up a song and it went like this: *Weeding for the Lord, weeding for the Lisa, 9-0, 9-0, 9-0.* I thought it sounded silly, my name in a song, weeding for me to score a 9.0, but it was kind of fun. So, I sang. As we pulled up ugly, dirty weeds and put them in a bucket, and dirt got all over my hands and under my fingernails, I was happy. I imagined the song and pulling those darn weeds was really positive stuff! I felt good inside. Of course, I didn't know if I'd score a 9.0 that coming meet, but with my mom's hearty burrowing and singing, and me sitting next to her, I felt this incredible energy, and I started to believe it was possible. My mom's voice trilled, she grinned and made yard work an adventure. Lisa's going to score a nine-oh! Woo-wee!

I knew scoring a nine was hard. I could not have believed it all on my own. But since my mom believed in me, I had faith. And this was typical. In all my training and competing, she was super positive. Even after something horrible would happen—I'd fall in a meet or sprain my ankle—my mom would say, "That's okay. We'll take care of it. Something good will happen next! You don't know when, but it will. You just have to *look* for it!"

And she was right! Good things always happened.

In my next competition, I walked in the gym and saw the trophy table. Oh my… they were shiny and pretty, and I wanted one! I had more motivation—to score a 9.0 *and* win a trophy, but ultimately, I didn't think about those things. I didn't think about the judges or my coaches, or competitors or the score, just doing my best technique and form…and trusting something good would happen. The beautiful memory of singing with my mom and believing success would come bolstered my confidence. So when I competed on floor, I felt my courage; there was an extra energy and spirit inside me. I loved gymnastics; I loved tumbling and dancing, and I loved competing.

That meet, I did a great floor performance. I hit every tumbling pass, leap, and turn; it was terrific! But when you walk off the mat, you don't know what score you'll get. I waited…I looked and waited… And there, flashed on the scoreboard, was a 9.05. I got a 9!

9.0

Wishing and Believing

Outside of practice, days or weeks before a performance, think of your wish. When you think about your desire, then tell someone. When you spend time being playful, talking or singing about your goal, that is putting time and effort into manifesting success. Do not underestimate wishing out loud for what you want. Or singing! When you take action, you are creating strong passionate emotions and self-belief. How you *feel* about reaching your goal gives you bodily

sensations—you'll feel alert, spirited, and more certain. That feeling is cause for what comes next; it is energy, and that is effective and powerful.

I will remind you, you can't control the officials or scores. You can't control who wins. But you can control your thoughts and attitude and that is *huge*. Create your words, phrases, and mantras. Say or sing repetitions of positive thoughts. Spend time with someone who believes in you. Listen to their upbeat messages since they believe you will achieve. That vitality will nourish your own spirit to believe. Then you can imagine specifically what you want, and you greatly increase your chances to make it come true. You do!

Hard Work Shapes Belief

On time to practice meant you were 10 min early; you were never late. We lined up like soldiers, at attention. We were drilled to perfection, conditioned till we cramped. If you were sick, you had to be really sick to miss practice, so "fake it till you make it" was the saying. Some called the gym a 'pressure-cooker'—no weaknesses allowed. But it worked. With constant group precision, sweat, and focus, we learned how champions prepare. At Utah, Greg Marsden was the best tough coach I ever had. He taught us diligence, true commitment, and the highest work ethic.

After double practices, muscles hurt like nothing else. I could barely walk, my legs ached so badly; it took forever to climb the six flights up to my dorm room. I carried my backpack, a gym bag, and two bags of ice for my ankles and knee. I iced while I ate or did homework. This was ceremonial. I was making the sacrifices…

Measuring and monitoring systems were in place, too, and extra monitoring to secure Greg's plan to be the best. We had physicals with the team doctor. Our trainers constantly checked our nagging injuries and administered treatments, daily, often twice a day. We got weighed in on random dates, we never knew when it was coming. And to be super exact, we had hydrostatic (underwater) weigh ins, which measured body composition, and most importantly, the percentage of fat you had. One team member had under 5% body fat. I was 10% that first year, and felt the pressure to improve. But it was essential to honor the process, accept the measuring, and accept the hard work. There was also strength testing, and bone density, and urine screenings, as well. Greg also knew when we were menstruating, because that effected our weight and performance. Nothing was sacred…yet the journey *was*.

We attended to and accepted every detail of training—flawless warm up drills, high-level skill development, flexibility, weight training and conditioning because we had the desire. My teammates and I wanted to win, too. But training was so tough, I wondered if I was good enough. I wondered, am I working hard enough? Hooey, that was doubt. I was good enough and I did work hard. I just had to practice patience and stay in the fight. Know that doubts would creep in. I learned to accept those too; it was part of the process of believing.

We also trained mentally. Dr. Keith Henschen taught us how to meditate to soft music, to attain a peaceful state through deep breathing and relaxation. We learned to get in tune with our calmest mind and body and know how to achieve it. We trained in mental imagery to "see" our best routines in competition. I saw myself on beam, so clearly, every hand movement, every flip was confident and easy. I saw my bar routine in slow motion, every position. I imagined a perfect floor routine and vault. All of it was real in my mind. Mental training became a full confirmation that success was coming. Seeing it and feeling it in my mind made me believe I could repeat it in a meet…any meet.

Months and months of training *developed* my ability to believe. This didn't happen in one practice or one month. Believing in the vision of winning nationals was cultivated over time. Through very hard work, shaping our bodies into top form, polishing our routines to excel, and doing mental imagery, we were manifesting. We had team talks that kept our focus on overcoming challenges, the process of competing well, not the results. And we spoke in detail about logistics, mats, boards, timing of every-thing to perform our best in competition. The plan to win was a mastermind of organization and actions. Mentally, we knew every single step to take. Working hard created a deep-seated sureness—to have no doubts and believe.

Mindset: Acceptance

Acceptance is to permit the reality of a situation, especially something uncomfortable; not resisting or trying to change the present situation. To understand processes, know there are ups and downs; embrace reality and trust that things will be okay.

Apply this mindset of acceptance. See reality. Accept a mistake and move on. Accept a crash or pain, then take steps to recover. When a coach disputes a score or a call by officials, it is your job to accept any outcome. If you lose after your best effort, accept the results, then learn from it. In relationships, observe yourself and other people. Accept your flaws and theirs. No one is perfect, we are all human. If someone is mean, you don't have to like them, but you also can't change them; you may have to tolerate a mean person, but talk to some-one wise to see if change is possible. Fighting is not the answer, so it's best to see reality and then think of options. If they are hurting you, then get help from someone you trust. Negative people will make it difficult for you to stay focused and in a positive mindset. You can consider strategies to change the situation, or not spend time around them, or focus on something else. But overall, when you practice acceptance of reality, this mindset allows you to be clear in your thoughts. You become wiser when you pause, don't react, and choose to stay calm. You can focus on putting energy toward being decisive and productive. You won't "fight" things you can't control, and you'll be able to train and perform your best.

The Possible Self

Now…what do you want? What do you want? That's the question. Declare it, then manifest and self-actualize who you want to become. Have you watched another athlete you admire? Do you imagine playing with strength and speed in the most incredible game? Do you think of racing faster than lightening? Maybe you dream of performing with perfection. But don't be someone else, be the best *you*.

I love the saying, "Anything is possible." You have incredible qualities and talent —you can do so many things! But all people create obstacles with worry and self-doubt. You think things will be too hard or won't work, so you limit yourself. But do you dream? Do you imagine your future self? What's happening in that dream, are you better than you are, today?

Think of your possible self. What will you be doing in the future? Use your powerful imagination. Remember, your mind has no limits. None! Swim in your own imagination and daydream about your future self and what you want to accomplish. It's inspiring! And that will be your guide.

Your Inspiring Room

To manifest success, a friendly positive environment is super important. What you see, hear, and touch affects you every day: colors, fun or inspiring items, your favorite books and music, encouraging messages, and especially, supportive and kind people. Athletes do best when they're surrounded with items they love, and especially, cheerful, confident voices and people. What do you surround yourself with? What is fun or meaningful to you? Do you have a good-luck charm, like a keychain, a pin, or band for

your wrist? Stuffed animals: I had many when I competed. Today, I have four furry friends who give me a smile and inspiration.

I also wear certain bracelets that have meaning to me; one has light blue beads and it reminds me of the ocean, and I love the beach! It fills my spirit and gives me energy. If you like tigers, perhaps a little tiger is on your desk. If you like purple, then I hope you have purple in your bedroom, or you wear purple clothes, or underwear! Whatever makes you happy, that is important!

Also consider where you spend time in your house. Is it nice and clean? Your bathroom, kitchen, family room…clean areas give a person energy. It's true. Organized space directly effects your mental space to rest, think, or be creative. Cluttered areas block productivity and actually clutter the mind; physical excess builds tension in you.

Now, think of the people in your life: your family, friends, teachers, coaches, even your dentist and doctor. When I was a kid, my dentist was totally into athletes and how they could get stronger and do awesome things. He thought I was a cool young gymnast in training; (I told him I wanted to go to the Olympics). He was excited for me, and going to the dentist reminded me that I was a hard-working athlete. That made me feel good! If you have a best friend who is interested in your sport, that's terrific. Whoever is positive in your life, try to spend time with them, or put up pictures of them in your room or locker. And…make a sign!

When you write and read a specific message, like "I am strong" that impacts you. You are telling yourself that you're strong, and like I said at the beginning of this book—you are the most important person in the world you will communicate with. Create positive messages! Make a sign! I coached a gymnast who did not like vault and didn't feel good about herself. She said she was not a vaulter. So we talked. I told her maybe it's hard, now, but she *will* get better. She *is* a vaulter; she just needs to stay focused and be persistent—not give up. I told her to go get paper and a marker. She did. I told her to make a sign: *I am a vaulter!* She made it. I said, "Post this sign in your room where you will see it every day. And believe it." So she put it on a wall in her room, and after three years it's still there. Over time, she has been dedicated and worked super hard. I will report, she has grown into a really great vaulter!

Kick-butt Practices and Exercises for Chapter 6

Exercise: Manifest, Manifest, 1, 2, 3…*and 4*

Step 1, Think: What do you want? Maybe you want to improve a move, or win your next game, or advance a level, make the All-Star team. These are common ideas. The thought is in your mind: I want… And there it is, be in tune with your desire.

Step 2, Say: Take it another step further. In conversation, an athlete will say in a determined voice, "I'm going to make the All-Star team." This may sound overly confident to some people. But when an athlete says what they want and what they *will* do, they are producing positive energy inside them. This is a voice of conviction. Speaking with conviction is an act of assertion. Say what you will do. Say what you will achieve. Tell someone. Who will you tell? With positive thoughts and words, you are self-actualizing. You are on the path to make it come true.

Step 3, Practice: Now apply hard work, especially when you feel tired and sore. It's uncomfortable to work hard. You sweat, cramp, and feel doubts. Accept it. Stay connected to your vision, to your goal. Surround yourself with positive people, and you're on the path to making it come true.

Step 4, Believe: This is the most challenging one…believing…or knowing. You need to practice 100% belief that your 'want' and 'will' is going to manifest into real life. Work hard, concentrate, and know the goal that you're working toward. For the athlete, imagine the full vision—for instance, you're on an All-Star team, wearing the team uniform, practicing with teammates, getting cues from the coach, traveling to away-games, playing for the team, and winning. See it. You are there. You are good enough. You are on the team, already.

Perhaps it's in your head right now, but your thoughts are positive energy! With this approach, your higher mind (your subconscious) acts as if you have it. You already have it. It is real. You see it, believe it, and know it. The best athletes in the world use this type of vision and mindset of 'believing' and 'knowing.' It's what makes them the best. You can do it, too. Imagine...and believe.

Exercise: Identify your Strengths and Weaknesses, Encourage Yourself

The better you know yourself, the better you can make choices and manifest what you desire. Answer questions as best you can. Consider talking to a trusted mentor, friend, or parent about this topic, and how they can support you in reaching your goals.

1. What do you see as your positives traits/character? What positive things do others say about you? (Example: I am thoughtful. I am determined.) Write 3 or more true statements.

2. What are your strengths in sports and on your team? What do others say? (Example: I'm a team player. I work hard.) Write 3 or more.

3. What does your doubting voice say to you? What do you say to yourself when you self-criticize? (Example: What's wrong with me. I'm not good enough.) It is very important to be aware of your negative thoughts so you can change them! Write 3 or more.

4. Practice reading and saying to yourself #1 and #2 lines—true positive statements.

5. Be aware of when the negative #3 statements enter your mind. Those stop you and create doubt. At that time, go back to the positive statements. Repeat them. If you don't encourage yourself, it will be difficult to believe... and to reach goals. Practice encouraging yourself!

Exercise: Create a Mental Tape or Mantra, Play it in your mind

Make up confident phrases that guide you into a calm, clear, and self-assured state. Like, "I am calm." Think, how do I want to feel? How do I want to play? Practice guiding yourself. Make a short list of 3-5 statements, and write them out. Design this mental tape and play it over and over. Breathe once for each line.

Example of Mental Tape:

I am calm (breathe).

I am strong (breathe).

I am focused (breathe).

I love to play (breathe).

Write your own, now. And when you repeat your words, you are centering yourself and connecting with your inner voice and inner strength. Practice repeating this mantra every night before bed. Every time you enter practice or a game. Make it a habit and you will be manifesting valuable emotions that lead to achievement.

Exercise: Scripting your Positions and Moves

Create a written script for each movement and skill you want to do, on the court, field, course, or in the water…any series of moves or a routine you do. Like an actor needs a script for speaking and moving on a stage, an athlete needs a script for thoughts and actions for your competition, game, or match. This keeps your mind busy, and keeps distracting thoughts away.

- Use one-word "cues," but keep it clear and relatable to your movements. Your script will include breathing, hand or foot movements, directions like, "relax" or "push" similar to a coach's positive instruction.

- For a golfer, maybe start with, "breathe, loosen my grip, get in rhythm, hit the target."

  A more precise version could be: "breathe, loosen, rhythm, target."

- For a diver, it could be: "breathe, step, step, high knee lift, jump tight, stretch up, clean pike, quick twist, open."

  A more precise version could be: "breathe, step, step, knee, jump, stretch, pike, twist, open."

As a reference, look back in chapter 5, "Fear" and see the illustration of the back handspring mental script for gymnasts. Include 'breathe' in your script, at first. When you get in a habit of taking a voluntary breath in your prep, then you don't have to think about it.

This scripting exercise should be repeated many times in your mind; 20 times in a practice is not too many. Do it for 30 days, a month, at least. Be intentional.

Keep practicing, use your script. It gives you a clear focus, awareness of your body, confidence, and it feels familiar. These produce best performances!

Exercise: Write it down, make a Sign!

A sign is concrete. No, not cement. But it is material, it's tangible. You can touch it. You can see it, read it, and it talks to you. It tells you what to do. It *reminds* you who you are and what you want. It confirms what you will achieve. Signs are awesome!

1. Get any size paper or art paper. Up to you. I suggest big enough that you can read it from across your bedroom.

2. Get markers or pens. Colors are great.

3. Make a Sign with a positive word or statement you like. You can use any of the phrases you've already written, like "I am strong," or create something fun, like "I will conquer!"

4. Put the sign where you will see it every day: on a wall in your room, or in the bathroom, or in your locker. I suggest a sign in your room, because it's good to see it before you sleep and when you wake up.

To Self-Actualize, Program your Mind

When you have an area of weakness, or there's a particular move you want to get, then program your mind for success. Programming your mind instructs your body, and that focus produces confidence. In gymnastics, one main element of vault is to get a powerful jump off the springboard. There is a spot on the board where the feet go. My team had struggled to jump on the "sweet spot"—a line on the board. The hesitation? One could over-jump and crash into the vault table and get injured. But the back of the board, there was little to no spring, so you had to really hit the sweet spot. The gymnasts needed help jumping on the line, and it seemed to be a psychological block. The task? Re-program the mind.

Exercise: Record your voice for Mental Focus

Use a recording device, maybe on your smartphone. Find a quiet spot and follow these instructions:

- Say and record what you want to do
- Say the statement multiple times
- Listen to it repeatedly—3 times a day, 6 days a week, for 2 weeks (minimum).
- Note: it typically takes a minimum 21 consecutive days to create a new habit. 60 days is common.

Record your voice saying each line:
I want…
I will…
I do…

Then listen. Listen to your voice recording, and visualize yourself doing the physical task. Feel it in your muscles. The speed. The power. Feel it in your bones! By speaking it, you tap into your personal power. You create the desired experience. It is real in your mind. Below is an example of a mental focus a baseball player might use: a batter facing a fast pitcher. But please create your own phrase. Note the emphasis on certain words — very important!

First series – I WANT

I want to step toward the pitcher.
I **want** to step toward the pitcher.
I want to **step** toward the pitcher.
I want to step **toward** the pitcher.
I want to step toward the **pitcher**.

Second series – I WILL

I will step toward the pitcher.
I **will** step toward the pitcher.
I will **step** toward the pitcher.
I will step **toward** the pitcher.
I will step toward the **pitcher**.

Third series – I DO

I step toward the pitcher.
I **step** toward the pitcher.
I step **toward** the pitcher.
I step toward the **pitcher**.

This method may seem tedious, saying and listening to such a message: "I step toward the pitcher, I step toward the pitcher, I step toward the pitcher…" Clearly redundant. But that is the point! Overdo! **To overdo is to immerse the mind in new thought.** In this way, neurons and synapses absorb sure-fire messages into the brain and transmit to the body. Repeating intention is like brainwashing…or brain *programming*. You are re-programming your mind. You have the power, but you must commit to it. If you are robotic, monotone, and not believing it—then it doesn't work. I encourage you to use a lively, determined voice. Grr!

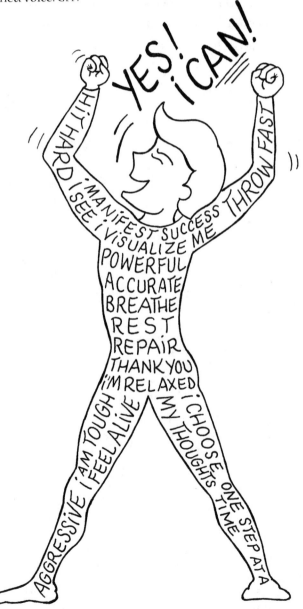

You are Your Thoughts

Here's a reminder: You create your reality with your thoughts. You manifest what you want. If you think, *I'm scared*, then you are scared; you will feel and act afraid. But if you change that thought to, *I can do this, I am brave*—even when you're feeling nervous, you can start to overcome. Your thoughts will guide you and you will begin to take positive actions.

Review your list of facts about yourself; positive truths. Realize mistakes happen. See it…without emotion…then move on. Say, "Anything is possible." Write it down. Post it on your wall, on your desk, on your mirror! Consider telling someone every day for a week. Say it with conviction and believe it!

Finally, say, "I create my reality." Repeat three times every day, to yourself, and write it down.

I create my reality

I create my reality

I create my reality

Chapter 7
Visualize, Visualize:
Slow Down, Dissect Skills,
See, Feel, and Hit

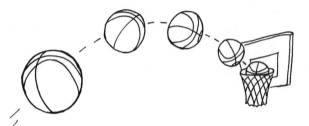

See the Ball

McKenna said, "I see the ball go through the hoop. I imagine a string that extends from my fingers, goes upward and curves back down to the net. When I shoot the ball, I imagine it goes from my fingertips, along the string, and right through the hoop."

This is my daughter. She had never visualized her shots before—until I coached her basketball team. I wasn't sure how it would go, my first time coaching basketball. But I focused on conditioning, getting down solid plays, and teaching mental skills. I taught them to believe in themselves through hard work, my confidence in them, and their successes in practices. We had team talks, jokes, and lots of laughs. I pumped them up, telling them they were strong and fierce. A major tool was, they learned how to visualize their free-throw shots. McKenna caught on, she liked it, and she practiced... That season, she scored a lot of points. Our entire team got into it, seeing their shots and being tough girls on the court. And the craziest thing...that team won the division championships. Visualizing helped.

I Might Crash

Alicia, a downhill skier, told me, "When I'm at the top of the hill ready to race, I get tense and nervous." "Why?" I asked, "What are you worried about?" She replied, "That I'll crash. I see myself going fast down the hill; I lose control, and then I crash… So I hold back."

"Do you *like* thinking about crashing?" I asked.

"No," she said.

I understood…there are risks, speed, and accuracy in racing downhill skiing. But the bottom line is to focus on what you *can* control; when you're standing at the gate, you *can't* control a future crash. That's wasted thought and negative energy.

So we worked on a new vision, not focused on success, or a time, and not thinking about crashing. Alicia learned to imagine taking that big hill of snow one gate at a time. She learned to see herself skiing while being in tune with her body. She could see and feel herself travel toward each gate slowly, and pass it with proper technique. In her mind, she gradually increased her speed with

SEE YOURSELF PERFORM WELL!!!

the same technique. Since skiing has other elements, air resistance and surface friction, Alicia practiced different scenarios of packed snow or powdered snow, windy or quiet air. She gradually learned to imagine herself racing at full speed and feeling confident with how she wanted to get low, lean to one side, and move in and out of each turn. You can choose to create a new positive picture in your mind; focused and in control. You can practice over and over, the mental repetitions in your mind. You can imagine success, even when you're nervous, and that vision grounds you and creates courage and poise.

What is Visualizing in Sports?

Visualization, or imagery, is a guided mental practice, recalling or creating pictures in your mind, involving sensory details. Self-guided, or with someone prompting, you can recall an experience, a specific performance in the past, or imagine something in the future. It's natural for athletes to recall mistakes and negative images—but that's not helpful. Learn to create positive images, and when you involve muscular sensations, emotions, and your other senses, like sound, taste, touch, and smell, the image is very real. What is known by sport psychologists is positive imagery can truly arouse muscle response and emotions like a real physical performance. Exact visualizing is so similar to reality that your brain doesn't know the difference. So training in imagery prepares you to play your best!

What you may not realize is that you visualize all the time, about school, food you want to eat, or friends you want to see…or don't want to see. This is not training, though. It's an everyday process and can often be sporadic and/or negative. Disciplined imagery, visualizing with precision and an intention to heighten your sports performance, gives you a great advantage. It's invaluable. You can condition your thoughts to be closely connected to your muscle activity during a move or play. When you visualize positive performances, you are strengthening that brain-to-muscle link that is vital for confident and accurate execution. Negative images, like the skier crashing, are common for athletes who do not rehearse successful movement and skills. But you can always correct images in your mind or form new ones. You are in control of your mind, no one else.

What do you imagine? When you practice "seeing" a correct move, you are plugged into what you can physically do. You let go of doubt and distraction and you live through your powerful imagination.

Your Brain is a Camera

When I coach workshops and individuals in mental training, I help athletes break down skills into parts—distinct body positions. The key when you visualize is to focus on what you see, and what you feel in your body, moment by moment. When you focus deeply on yourself, you slip into your own "dream world," as if reality is suspended and you momentarily live in a bubble. I was talking to one of my athlete-clients, Sophia. She was having trouble focusing, and she was nervous about performing. I said, "Create a private world—your own bubble. A Sophia-bubble. In your bubble, nothing else exists. It's only you, feeling your breath, seeing, and feeling your body moving. Nothing else exists." She nodded, okay. Getting into a dream world gave Sophia permission to let go of the outside world—expectations, scores, voices, and distractions. She relaxed more, practiced visualizing her moves step-by-step, and she was able to mentally zoom into her performance. Her level of concentration increased, and she did great!

To learn how to visualize, think of your brain functioning like a camera. A camera doesn't think. A camera doesn't talk. It just sees. A camera takes a photo of an image, or a moving image, and your brain can do the same thing. When you hold a position for two seconds, and you pay attention to what you see and feel, "click!" your brain takes a mental "picture" of that position. You can do this in any sport, and the best place to start is with a basic move. Break down any simple move into poses, and let your mind be a camera. Notice and see your hands: Are they low, medium, high? Are they in front of me, at my side, or behind me?

When you practice a mental sequence in s-l-o-w m-o-t-i-o-n, seeing through your mind's eye and feeling your body in each position, you are training mentally. You are imprinting exact movements in your mind: a master plan of what you will do. At the end of the chapter, there are steps to follow.

Beginner's Mind

When I work with athletes, I talk about using Beginner's Mind. It's all about mentally slowing down, being in tune with accuracy in the mind and body, and getting away from rushing through moves. Beginner's Mind means to be open to a situation or skill, like it's your first time learning it or doing it.

Do not hold onto a prior idea, like "This is hard," or "This is easy." Let go of thoughts, intuition, and judgment. You are beginning…it's completely new…slow down.

When you want to hone your ability, and connect to exact technique, then use Beginner's Mind. In your sport, select a basic move. For instance, basketball players may choose a free-throw shot. Golfers, a short putt. Tennis players, a straight forehand. Gymnasts, a handstand. You will start new and think about what a coach has told you when learning how to do it. What was the instruction, moment by moment? Writing it out helps organize the process in your mind. Again, this is training your mind to slow down and not rush through important positions. Basics are key to start with, then you can advance into higher level skills and plays.

Give yourself ten minutes to dissect a skill and get very specific. See the next illustration for an example…it's a profile view. There are no words. Just positions. Get in tune with the 'camera' in your brain, what you see. In your sport, choose a simple move, break it down, and start visualizing. Drop previous experiences from your mind and start new so you can open yourself to your highest potential. Now, I'd like to introduce you to a new mindset…

Mindset: Letting Go

Letting go is a practice in releasing a previous image, thought, or emotion; you can express and drop tension, discomfort, or fear. Then decide what's next: *I will adjust. I will heal. I will repair.* You can intentionally put mental clutter in the past, throw it in the trash, choose a new focus in the the present moment, and move toward what you want.

One of my coaches used to say, "Drop it at the door." He wanted us athletes to mentally let go of any 'life issues' before entering the gym, and to focus solely on practice. I liked this 'letting go' image of dropping a bag of mental stuff. And…if I wanted to…I could pick it back up when leaving the gym.

Slow Down and Let Go of Results

When athletes are driven, it's common for minds to race. You feel rushed, nervous, unfocused. I know, I know, you want results! Well, when you slow down in life, stress lessens and things become clearer, even easier. When you slow down in sports, mentally, you will feel more in control. Movements will be more accurate and you'll feel very confident. In this chapter, I share techniques to help you slow down a skill in your mind, or a series of moves, step by step.

When you slow down physical actions in your mind:

· you heighten awareness of your mental and emotional status

· increase ability to manage your thoughts and feelings

· become more in tune with the state of your body—tense or relaxed

· connect to being more technically accurate in your movements

· and gain a strong sense of being more in control.

To master your mind and body, start with slowing down. You will see more clearly how to put your body in correct positions, and you can move from one position to the other in a sequence. It's helpful to bring in sensory details, like the texture of a ball or bat, the sound of a ball bouncing, a whistle, a crowd applause, and maybe the smell of popcorn. You can control your mind and body together by preparing yourself through visualizing.

Sight Can Hinder You: Develop your Inner Vision

Your eyesight connects you to what is—physical reality—what is real in the world. Many things are amazing through sight: You watch an Olympic athlete jump higher or race faster than ever before. An eagle soars across the sky with incredible grace and freedom. Or a pink and orange sunset illuminates the sky and peacefulness washes over you… Sight is a gift. Yet when it comes to your own performance in sports, sight can hinder you and cause problems.

Many athletes look at their opponent and immediately feel intimidated: a "perfect" body, someone super fast, or they just look confident! Or, maybe you see a judge and worry they will be too hard on you. Or you see a tough team and instantly you feel nervous—they're tall, or super muscular, or they have that killer face, like you're in trouble because they are definitely going to win. Finally, have you looked at the scoreboard and it shows that you're behind, or the other team is ahead? Of course you have, and seeing the numbers starts to affect you.

Sight is a constant stimulant. It's in your face all the time. You see things and then interpret them into an idea about good or bad, winning or losing. Your sight distracts you from *you*. So…external vision can highjack your brain from focusing on what's important. In essence, sight overpowers your mind. It effects your thoughts, distorts your perspective, and it limits your imagination. Everything we see can easily distract us from our inner mind, from being in tune with your own abilities and performance.

Inner vision allows you to 'see' more and imagine more. Do you like to imagine great things? Because the truth is your mind has *no limits*. You can imagine anything! The key is to develop your inner vision. Be aware of your thoughts and feelings, know when it's critical to view the outside world, observe, and know when it's time to go inside to your inner world, observe yourself. Co-function with both the external and internal. As you learn and practice switching back and forth, you can increase your mental focus and elevate your physical movements. You may even become a master.

Are You the Audience or a Player?

Audience: When you sit in the stands, you observe others. You watch athletes on a track, a court, or gym. You are an audience member watching them. Can you imagine from the stands, seeing yourself play sports? From a distance, you watch yourself play a game or swim a race, you can see yourself from the view of an audience member. I call this third person, like watching yourself on a screen.

Player: Now, consider you are not in the stands, you are in the game or competition. You are a player, and you see other players on the field through your eyes. You see your hands, arms, and legs extending from your torso. You look down and see your feet on the ground beneath you. You feel your fingers wrap around and grip a bat or golf club. You feel your feet inside your socks and shoes. And when you think about it, you feel yourself inhale…and exhale… You're inside your body. This is first person.

When you visualize, you can see yourself from either view. **Most powerful is first person, inside your body, because you can elicit the sensation of your muscles in action and responding.** You can recall or create the vision of being in a game, amongst coaches, an opponent, and officials. This simulates real experiences in competition. When you break down skills and use a script, first person is most beneficial to become accurate in your moves. If you use a "screen" and watch from the audience, that's helpful too. But I encourage you to get inside your body and see from your own eyes while doing your imagery and mental training.

Make Mental Corrections

When you visualize a performance, you live it. And you can make corrections in your mind, too, because in your mind, there are no limits! If I say the words, purple cow, then you are likely imagining a purple cow. Imagine a pencil on a table top. Imagine it moves across the table and stops at the edge. Did it go slowly…or quickly? It's your decision. You can imagine anything. So when you see yourself performing in your mind, you can imagine going higher, faster, or slower…and hitting every correct position. A baseball player can imagine a home run. A football player outruns the defense and makes a touchdown. And if you make a mistake in your mind, that's okay. Freeze yourself like a statue right at the point of the mistake; then in your mind, in slow motion, correct the move. Move to the right, or left, or any direction. You can do this, it just takes practice. I learned how to do it when I was a teenager and was struggling—I was deathly afraid of my skills after a terrible fall. If you read "The Crash" in Chapter 2, you'll understand how I could not visualize any skills I had done for years. But I learned and practiced imagery, and gradually, I was able to see and feel myself doing gymnastics again. In your sport, you can, too!

★ Kick-butt Practices and Exercises for Chapter 7 ★

Exercise: Dissect a Skill, Take Mental Pictures...

Choose a basic skill for your sport. For gymnasts, dissect a handstand, step down to lunge; for a basketball player, break down a free-throw shot into separate parts; for a diver, observe a step-by-step simple forward dive; for a golfer, an easy putt. A basic move.

1. Slice the skill into 4 to 6 parts, like cutting a pizza into slices. You can create a mental photo of each part (slice) of a skill. Be specific. For athletes in water or on snow, like a diver, swimmer, ice skater, or skier, use mats and blocks on land to hold yourself in poses.

2. You can write down names of the positions—a short script: like, "stand, swing, jump, pike, extend, land." (See Chapter 5, specifically the illustration of the gymnast doing a back handspring in distinct positions with a script—a word or two words for each posture.)

3. You can even draw stick figures; artists not required. No worries, it's fun! (Don't be so serious.)

4. Immerse: Immerse yourself into each part of your skill, like you're learning it for the first time—beginner's mind. Focus on *feeling* your arms, if they are straight, slightly bent, more bent; *notice* your hips, if they're open all the way flat, hyper extended into an arch, or slightly rolled forward into a hollow position. Notice. This process ingrains positions into your mind, the exact positions, and you can let go of detracting thoughts.

5. After you plan out a series of positions for your basic move, prepare to physically do the skill two times. Again, if you are on land, but train and compete in water, on ice or snow, just do one position at a time on land. If you need a coach to help, ask. And say 'please.'

6. Speak your intention: Before each turn, take a breath and tell yourself, "I will focus on what I see and feel in each position." This is setting your mind to focus.

7. Recall: After you perform the skill, pause, close your eyes, take a deep breath, and recall what you just did. "See" in your mind each part...each position. Finish with success.

8.   If it doesn't go well the first time, that's okay! It's common for the mental rehearsal to be bumpy at first or unclear. That's fine. Repeat the skill physically, one part at a time, then pause…and recall, again.

It can take anywhere from twenty to one hundred mental repetitions to start to get it exactly how you want it in your mind. Don't give up. Keep seeing your skill. Keep visualizing.

Exercise: Relaxed Imagery in Bed

When you are getting ready for sleep at night, doing visualization in bed is perfect. *Perfect!* At the end of the day, getting fully relaxed, quiet, and calm allows you to have the clearest images in your mind. There are no distractions, you can release all muscle tension and get immersed into your dream world. Plus, this optimistic vision before sleep nurtures your spirit, and prepares you for what you want to do the next day, or in your next practice or game. This is very powerful.

1.   Before you start, decide what you will rehearse in your mind: a skill on the court, field, or in a gym, during practice? Or will you perform in a competition or race? I suggest you do imagery for 5-10 minutes, including breathing and relaxing your body. And I recommend first person; you are in your body, doing the moves.

2.   Lie in bed. Get cozy. Use the exercises, *Breathing and Relaxing*, from Chapter 2.

3.   Go through each step, and remember in breathing and relaxing to fill your lungs all the way, fully expand your abdomen, and exhale all the way out, slowly… Let your muscles go soft and heavy…sink into the bed.

4.   Create a mental ritual: Include your thoughts and actions just before your performance. A preparation of sorts that you can make as part of a routine: A ritual, a pre-performance routine, helps to set your mind on the task, and gets you very focused in your inner world.

5.   Visualize yourself in slow motion or regular speed, doing your skills and plays. Repeat each one at least 5 times. Five mental repetitions.

6.   Use sensory detail: Imagine the tactile experience of your hands and feet touching or swinging. Imagine the temperature—is it warm or cold? Include sounds and smells—pine trees, grass, water splashing, chlorine, chalk, audience noises, etc.

7. Practice nightly: You will refine your imagery with frequency. After a few
    weeks or more, your brain will get familiar with the images, you'll feel
    muscles reacting in your mind's eye, and it will be distinct. The skills will be
    very clear with no mistakes and you will also see your surroundings and
    hear noises. As it becomes more vivid, three repetitions is fine.

Exercise: Prepare for Mistakes and Surprises

Too many times, athletes are surprised. Awful things happen in competition.
You experience a fall or weird crash you weren't expecting. An opponent made
a move you didn't see coming. How do you deal with it? You need to prepare…
prepare for *everything*.

1. See yourself in a competition or game, and imagine the hardest
    circumstances. If you play outside, bad weather, cold, wind, rain, a slippery
    field or ball. If it's inside, consider poor equipment, horrible crowds, unfair
    officials, bad-mouth opponents.

2. Write out several scenarios, imagine yourself in each terrible circumstance.
    See yourself breathing calmly.

3. Use positive encouragement, like: "I can handle it." "Slow down and be
    smart." "Trust my body." "I'm strong and prepared."

4. See yourself go through moves and plays, experiencing difficulties on the
    outside, but you are zoomed in mentally and totally focused on your body's
    movement, step-by-step.

5. Feel your muscles in action. Feel your own determination. You *like* a
    challenge. You *want* to overcome.

When you practice this type of vision, facing obstacles that are extremely hard,
you will not be as surprised when something really happens in a competition
or game. You will recover quickly and play mentally at a higher level than your
opponent. You will be tougher.

Believe it.

Chapter 8
Speak Honestly, Create True Partnerships, Build a Team

"Words are powerful," I've said, and they are. In this book, you've been learning positive ways to imagine *yourself* and talk and listen to *yourself*—the most important person in your whole life! Now, I'll share advice, stories, and ideas about interacting with others. Listen to their messages. Welcome their sure energy. Share your true thoughts and vitality with *others*.

Used wisely, words, spoken or written, are a gift over and over. We remember them, and they rest and stay in our mind for a long, long time.

Guys, Use Words and Make 'em Count

Boys of all ages have thoughts and feelings, but behavioral science has confirmed that you're different than females who tend to talk and share more—guys are more about action and motion. True. So words are going to be brief. On that note, make them count. You can learn how sharing the truth, versus putting on your tough-guy-mask, makes a bigger impact. If you want to achieve, if you have goals, you need to be wise, and on some level, connect verbally and emotionally with your coach; if you're on a team, connect with your teammates. If you are disconnected or aloof, then you will lack the combined positive energy that boosts confidence and performance. So this is not a light suggestion, it's important. Consider young men on college and pro teams—the best characteristics lie in the closeness of the teams. The coach-athlete relationship is key, and the players often admire, respect, and appreciate each other—and tell each other.

Notice top players in your sport. It's common for these athletes to bond with their coaches and support team: trainers, strength coaches, nutritionists… They know and trust them. Because no athlete does it alone. And when people keep showing up for you, they matter. So give a high-five when you arrive and leave. Offer a compliment on their effort. Say, "Thank you" for anything and everything, "How are you?" and "Hey, how can I help?" Look them in the eye, don't look down and utter in passing. Give them your attention. Those thoughtful actions and words connect you to each other and produce a joint spirit that is more powerful than you know. Read this chapter and see if you can strategize more. Because words are powerful.

Notes Inspire

On my club team, I was the focused one. Usually in a mental tunnel, thinking about my next turn, my next skill, driven to do better in my next meet. I never cheated on conditioning, I did every repetition I was told to do. Training was serious. But I also loved my team and we talked and laughed on our breaks. We travelled and competed together, shared hotel rooms, ate at restaurants, sang loudly to Pat Benatar songs, like "Hit Me With Your Best Shot," and we just loved each other. Through the years, I learned that some of the girls appreciated my hard work in the gym; I inspired them. And others had done the same for me. We all cheered for each other and gave each other good luck cards and gifts for meets.

One teammate wrote me a terrific 'good luck' letter when I was heading to a big competition. Her letter meant so much to me, because I didn't know how she truly saw me or felt about me. Her words gave me a boost of love and confidence that was invaluable in my sports life… Here is part of her letter:

Dear Lisa,

I'm sorry I can't go to your meet on Saturday, but I'm going to try real hard to come on Sunday to give you some support! I'll be praying for you. I'm so glad we are friends because you are a lot of fun to be with. I've known you for a long time and you have always worked hard! You have earned everything you've gotten and I'm so happy for you! Lisa, if you do the job in the meet, like you do in the gym there is no doubt in my mind that you will make it! And after elite comes the Olympics!

Love ya,
Valorie

The Power of Written Words

Has anyone written a letter like that to you? Or have you composed and given one to a teammate? Maybe for guys, send a short text to a teammate: "Let's win this thing!" This can rouse fun and excitement. And written words take effort, have meaning, and can sometimes be better than talking. You can read a letter and put it down, then pick it up again and re-read it. Think about it… The writer is not in front of you, so you aren't thinking about what you want to say next. You're simply absorbing their thoughts and feelings. It's a favor to receive supportive notes; from teammates, parents, friends, even coaches, written notes are powerful. They create a bond and the ability to see more deeply into the person who wrote it, and see deeper into yourself. Consider writing to your teammates or anyone you care about. You'll be sharing yourself, deepening an important relationship and giving them your good energy.

Teammates, Teammates: Like Family

There's no better partner than a wonderful teammate; they are the closest in going through the same experiences as you. But it's easy to make assumptions about their family life, or struggles outside of sports, unless you ask. So be curious. Be kind and very supportive. You are truly significant in each other's lives. Maybe you feel like brothers or sisters, sometimes. Because you are shaping each other and will always remember. In the hardest practices, the shared trust between you is like magic in getting through painful conditioning, tough drills, or a coach's frustration. I know, because I've been there, and I couldn't have done it alone. My teammates are like my family…and still are.

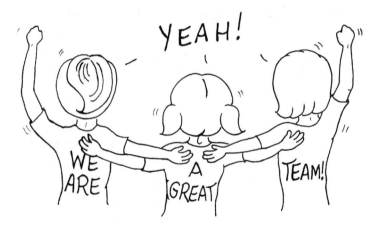

Meetings with Open Minds

To overcome obstacles and tough opponents, and then rise to the top, team meetings are essential. Talking and listening to each other is the heart of the process. If your team does all physical work but no true human connection, you will lack the vital character of knowing each other, caring about the group's mission, and trusting you're all working very hard, together. So be honest—share your thoughts.

1. Team Meetings—Teammates Only (no coach)

Do you ever sit down with your teammates and talk real-talk? Serious talk? Are you hesitant to open up about a problem? Here's some advice: Stay connected to the team's mission and desire to achieve; that will help keep the members working together. When you express *your* wish to work hard and reach the group's goal, then people will appreciate you.

If you have a problem ask for help, because *everyone struggles*. Maybe on different levels, some more, some less, but everyone faces challenges. It's not complaining if you keep it honest and brief. Again, speak in facts about what's happening. Ask for ideas and help in a positive voice, because you want to resolve it and make the team great.

Example 1: "My ankle keeps bothering me. I've iced and tried everything. I don't want coach to think I'm faking. Does anyone have a suggestion?"

Teammates' answers: "I go to a sports doctor, you can get the number." Or, "Maybe ask coach for a couple days to rest it. Injuries get worse if you keep playing on them."

When injured, consider helpful adults; it's usually smart to talk your parents and maybe there's an assistant coach. But even a team captain could aim you in the right direction. And there's always the internet. I give resources in the last chapter, so take a look. .

Example 2: "I can't get that play in practice, we're moving so fast. Coach wants it down, and so do I. I want to get it, quickly, but I'm not sure how."

Teammates' answers: "I can show you." Or, "Ask the assistant coach, he'll help you."

Someone may offer tips or they might help you before or after practice. And most importantly, you all need to support each other. When you listen to each other and show empathy—that you understand the problem and care—that's huge. When teammates care, a sense of personal power will rise. Because you are not alone, and your collective energy will continue to make you a better team. So speak up.

2. Team Meetings with Coach

The best coaches facilitate clear, patient conversation amongst team members, suggesting everyone takes a turn talking. That creates a wonderful team dynamic; everyone matters. And since all coaches are in a position of power—they are the leader—it can be difficult to speak up when you're afraid you might not say 'the right thing.' The key is to bond with your teammates through hard work and honesty. Treat everyone with respect. That gives you a voice, and they will want to hear your thoughts. If your coach is encouraging and typically positive, I would bet he or she is willing to consider how to help you and your teammates.

Discussing practices or games, be honest.

Example 1: "On defense, I'm doing my best, but other teams keep scoring. It makes me mad and I want to change that."

Example 2: "I keep getting open, but I'm not getting the ball so I can score. Can someone pass to me or talk about our strategy?"

Example 3: "It doesn't sound good when players make negative comments. If we want to win, we need to be together and not criticize anyone. Let's stay focused on the game."

These examples point to problems *and* the desire to improve. A team member can start real discussion that has impact on others. It will be awkward at times, because someone may feel accused for not trying. But if no one speaks up, then nothing gets resolved. The emphasis needs to be on the team's issues and concentrating on finding solutions, together. Keep to the facts, don't blame or say mean things. On and off the field, respect is imperative. If you are brave to speak, others will be brave, too. Remember: Your voice matters. You matter. And your coach is eager to have athletes who care, who contribute, and who have integrity. Those qualities, in addition to hard work, are signs of great athletes, and…a great team.

Every athlete and team goes through uncomfortable meetings and struggles. Players get confused and sometimes feel alone. But the best athletes and teams look for solutions and learn to rebound. It's helpful to take time to process and not react…but think… After a problem or a loss, great teams rise. They learn to be strong internally when things are tough. They are resilient. This is the final mindset for you…

Mindset: Resilience

Resilience is a personal choice to recover promptly from adversity. To rebound after setbacks, injuries, difficulties. You rise after a fall and bounce back after a mistake. You decide to refocus after confusion or failure. To be resilient is to make an intentional shift into positive thinking after a negative experience.

Spend time with your peaceful, authentic self...

Be Authentic

People respond to authenticity. Because when you're real—not faking or hiding—you are fully human, and you are trustworthy. Coaches and team-mates feel they can count on you; they believe you have integrity to tell the truth. I know speaking honestly is not always easy. We're afraid of being judged. But when you work hard and strive to reach your goals, you vibrate and send out positive energy. When you are authentic, people will understand. Be real even when you're vulnerable; that's not being weak, it's being honest about a struggle, and you will work through it. The key to authenticity is honest, clear, and respectful communication, whether it's in good times or hard times. So spend time with yourself, visit your peaceful, calm mind… think of what's true for you. Feel good about being true to yourself and honest with others. That is confidence… and wisdom.

Three-Hour Meeting

It was silent… And we couldn't leave the hotel room until we all spoke and we cleared the air. It was another meeting for our Utah team. Talking, listening, and being very honest were the pillars for success throughout the year. It was my senior year, and getting to know each other intimately and learning how to work together meant getting uncomfortable sometimes. We were on a trip in Arizona, and there were rumblings or something. Jealousy, anger, fear, the team not doing well, it was something, because we were lacking that fabulous poise and harmony. Greg, our coach, believed in very open communication, which sometimes hurt. Being respectful was a core value of his: have no secrets and face all issues, even the unpleasant ones. Put it out on the table and deal with it.

Where meetings usually took an hour, this one dragged out. In the hotel room, there were eleven of us spread out in a small space, and every single person had to share something deep; either about the team or their own personal struggle. It was hard. No one wanted to be negative, depressing, or point a finger. But being "nice" was not okay. You had to be real.

We sat quietly as people got up the nerve to talk. That was not easy, waiting for someone to be brave and speak. We sat, looked at each other…looked at our fingernails… But each girl took a turn. One after another, each team member opened up, and we all listened. We understood…and we cared. There were a few tears, but we were going to be okay. In fact, almost immediately afterward, it felt like the air had literally been cleared. As we walked out, we gently touched each other on the shoulder or back or gave a hug. No doubt about it, we were going to be great.

It's hard being vulnerable in front of everyone. But the strength of our team was getting through 'the hard,' because we planned on doing great…we all wanted to win.

Whether you're on a team, or you're a solo athlete with a coach, my message for you is to get comfortable with being *uncomfortable*. Even in a 20-minute meeting, realize a long silence can be difficult while waiting for someone to speak. Don't fill the silence just because no one's talking. Take a breath. Trust in the silence. Believe the words will come. And it will be okay.

Don't Hide

It's common for many of us to hide our feelings, put up a front and look cool. Especially in practice: follow the coach's instructions, suck it up, be "positive." Which is good. You gotta get through hard practices to improve. But when you're injured or struggling to perform, it's not wise to hide reality—you can make it worse. Plus, any negative thoughts, pain, and confusion, will affect others around you.

Part of your job is to learn about yourself, learn *how* to be tough. And the other part is to communicate when you're really struggling. Because hiding the truth (a recurring injury or a terrible fear) is not being wise. Learn the difference between a tweaked ankle and a badly jammed or hurt ankle. If you can't 'shake it off' in a few minutes, then get help.

Coaches and teammates seek *inner power,* because they need strong, high performers. When you find the right moment to speak with truth, respect, and thoughtfulness, coaches will see you as a mature and committed athlete.

Create Partnership with Open Communication

To reach your goals, a positive partnership requires open communication. Say what's important to you. Say what you want. Say what's real. Of course, listen, too. Really listen with patience and curiosity. Respect and take guidance from your coach and parents, *and* be a participant in the conversation. *Par-ti-ci-pate.*

Be part of the team plan, or your own plan, if you are an individual athlete. Don't follow blindly without thinking. You have an intelligent mind. You have thoughts and feelings. It's important for you to contribute and be part of your development and shape your success.

Advocate for yourself and be honest:

"Put me in, coach! I can do it!"

"I'm off, today. Nothing feels right. Can we make another plan?"

"I feel confident with these plays. I know I can score."

Let the coach *know* about you.

If You are Shy

If you are always quiet, your coach will make guesses. He/She can't read your mind and can't tell how you feel by looking at you. Body language speaks, but not completely. As smart and observant coaches can be (and I trained with the best), they don't read minds. So, get help to talk to your coach. A family member, a team captain, or an assistant coach can communicate honestly and clearly so your head coach learns about you. Help your coach see the best options according to your mindset, talent, an injury, how you feel that day. If you have specific desires, your coach won't know unless you tell them. It's very important that you get help to speak up.

To help yourself reach out for support, get into a calm space in your mind and body. Take a few moments and tune into your breath and body and feel peaceful. Self-Advocate from a place of authenticity and speak from your heart.

Or…Write a Letter to Coach

Finally, if being in the coach's presence seems nerve-wracking or daunting, even with another person there for support (a parent, teammate, or assistant coach), then write a note. Think what you'd like to say and make a draft. When you write a letter, you have all the time to consider your words and what's truly on your mind. When you speak, you are often wondering what the other person is thinking, which is distracting. You will still honor and respect your coach by being assertive and thinking things through. Your coach will be able to read it, "hear" your voice, think about it, and  not need to react or respond immediately. Your coach can put down the letter, re-read it, and later, after thinking, he/she can thoughtfully respond to you.

If You Don't Feel Safe

If a coach criticizes or yells only at you, or a coach embarrasses you in front of others as if joking, this is difficult. So get help.

If a coach threatens you in any way, or touches you or says anything that seems inappropriate, *then you need major help.*

Do not wait for the right moment. Immediately get in touch with another adult you trust, and ask if you can talk with them in private.

I'M HAVING A PROBLEM... CAN I TALK TO YOU?

It can be difficult to talk about a situation where you're scared that you'll be judged, or told that you are exaggerating. If a coach says, "You're making a big deal out of nothing," but it feels like a big deal to you, then talk to another adult. If you feel nervous, frightened, or worried, then it's important to take steps to feel safe. Most coaches do not want to hurt an athlete or their team. They are coaching to create positive experiences. Most coaches want to build up athletes to become strong and learn how to win. But some coaches are not like that; some are critical, negative, tear you down, and do not change—that's their style. In that case, you may want to rethink being on that team, or getting coached by that person.

A smaller number of coaches misuse their position. They intimidate athletes. Even cross the line into abuse. When an athlete is scared of the coach, then that coach and position needs to be challenged.

No athlete should ever feel unsafe or scared of getting hurt in any way by the coach.

When you open up and share what's happening and how you're feeling, you will feel supported. You can listen to a caring adult and understand all your options, and then choose a better direction for yourself. Or if action is required to stop a coach from hurting you or others, a trusting adult can help consider options.

Kick-butt Practices and Exercises for Chapter 8

Exercise: Be Authentic for an Hour

Who are you when no one else is around? When there's no TV, phone, iPad, or computer? Do you read? Do you take a nap? Do you water plants, draw, listen to music, write…? Do you create anything? Who are you? Be your authentic self for an hour once a week for one month. Nurture a plant or garden. Take a long bath or shower and soothe your skin. Research and dream of a trip you'll take some day—to another country! Observe your thoughts while you do something creative. If you like yourself, then you will enjoy being with yourself. And that's who your coach and teammates will trust. The real you.

Exercise: Actively Listen…

In a conversation, you're usually halfway listening, and halfway *thinking* of what you want to say. Have you heard of *active listening*? This means fully being curious about the person, what they are saying and how they are feeling. This is also a heart exercise. Caring about one another. But mostly this is an excellent chance to improve your communication skills.

1. Ask someone you trust to do a short activity with you. A listening exercise.

2. Sit about 2 feet apart in a room that is quiet. Face each other. Look at each other.

3. Set a timer for 2 minutes

4. One person takes a turn and talks about something, anything, their dog, a dream they have, anything…the other person is listening and NOT responding. Maybe they nod their head or smile, but they can not talk.

5. After the two minutes end, switch roles. Now the talker is the listener, and the listener is the talker.

6. Set the timer for 2 minutes, again.

7. Repeat exercise—one person speaks for 2 minutes and the other fully listens, not responding, except silent reactions with their eyes and face.

You are both taking a turn at being in a moment of open-mindedness as you listen. You both notice body language and facial expressions. You are fully listening. Like watching a movie, you are totally caught up. So…with a parent, friend, teammate, or other family member, practice listening! To be a good communicator, people think talk talk talk. But good listening is a skill.

Practice: Visualize The Talk

If you're going to have a serious talk with a parent, coach, or
someone important, you can visualize it. Imagine you are
sitting with them and how you'd like it to go. Imagine what
they might say, and how you can respond. Think of what you'd
like to say, plan it out, and consider their response. See yourself being calm…
breathing…and feeling good about sharing your thoughts, working things out
and taking steps to resolving a problem. Visualizing can truly prepare your
mind to be open, to speak clearly, and to be forgiving if there are hard feelings. This takes 5 minutes and you can even write down some notes after you
visualize, to remind you what to say. Remember, you can manifest success in a
conversation, too!

Exercise: Write a Letter to Your Coach

1. Be authentic. Say what's important to you, what you desire.

2. Be open. Reveal your obstacles with facts, not emotions; point out struggles
    and/or concerns from the "I" point of view. Ex: "I'm struggling with…" Don't
    point the finger at someone else. Only talk about yourself. And yes, this is
    vulnerable yet very, very wise.

3. Offer any suggestions you might have to collaborate and move in the
    direction you'd like.

4. Acknowledge. Point out that you value your coach's ideas, philosophies,
    rules.

5. Be warm and gracious. Say 'thank you' to your coach for taking the time to
    "listen," understand, and help you.

6. Brief. Keep it as brief as possible. It helps to get to the point and not
    over-speak.

7. End with gratitude for any time your coach can give you.

8. Deliver the letter with a smile, and have no expectations for a good result.

9. Accept. Know you did your best in communicating your needs to your
    coach and accept *any* outcome. Remember, you can't control your coach.
    Only yourself. So keep practicing being your *highest self*, no matter what.

Fun Bonding: Team Party or Hike, Take Pics, Laugh

If your team hasn't done a fun activity away from practice or games, make a suggestion to your team, team captain, or coach. It's important to experience your teammates and coach outside of the sports atmosphere. Get to know their personalities.

Idea 1: Suggest a team party at someone's house, a park, or a pizza place. Play music, eat delicious food, play games.

Idea 2: Go on a hike in nature, or an urban hike in the city. Gather items you find or purchase and put them in your locker or in a team locker room.

Take pictures of each other, put the photos up on a board and celebrate your team. If you can do this at least once, or maybe a couple times a year/season, that's terrific! You'll talk and laugh and get to know each other in a totally different way, bond into a closer group, be a more dynamic team. Together, you may even feel like you can conquer the world.

Team Exercise: Chemistry

For a team meeting, suggest to your teammates that you do something to increase the team's chemistry and workability. A simple and fun exercise—each team member shares a childhood story, or an unusual occurrence in their life. It's not required, but if the coach can join in, that's great! He or she can also share a story, and it's often funny and very surprising when you all learn personal gems about each other. Again, you will continue to deepen the bond and trust between you. This makes a powerful, and sometimes a magical, team.

Team Exercise: What I Like—Boost Team Confidence

This exercise is an open expression in noticing someone's qualities and their value on the team. It's important to take this seriously—not just laugh—because the intent is to boost the confidence of each player, and likewise, the team. You can do this at a team dinner or team gathering. Sit in a circle, and one at a time each member shares positive thoughts about the two team members sitting to their left; what qualities they have, their personality and strength on the team, and anything else you notice about them. This really is an amazing practice. More than physical workouts, when you open up and state someone's value, they hear it. And as I said…Words are Powerful!

Team Exercise: Who Is It?

In a team meeting, everyone can write on a small piece of paper a private fact about themselves. Something you're pretty sure no one knows. Fold up all the papers and put them in a hat. Each team member can draw out one at a time. One member, or team captain (or coach) can read the note aloud, and everyone can take turns guessing who it is. This is super fun!

Examples:

1.   I built the best blanket forts with my brothers.

2.   I threw-up in class in first grade.

3.   I was Captain America for Halloween.

4.   If it were possible, I'd meet and share a meal with Ghandi.

Team Exercise: The Team Goal

This is fun and simple! Discuss what you all want to achieve as a team. Take turns talking. Ask each other, What do you think? and listen. When thinking of a team goal, consider the level of competition, the level of your team's abilities, and always be positive. Make two goals—the ultimate goal that seems like a big dream; then come up with another achievement that sounds more realistic. Live in the mindset of the dream. Post a cool sign or picture of a winning photo or championship trophy in your locker room, even in your bedroom. You will rise through your team spirit. And maybe you will actually manifest it!

Chapter 9
Competition Mindset

I love to win. In fact, I want to win all the time. But we only control ourselves, we can't control our opponent, teammates, or the officials. And…winning is a result. So, for your highest mind and best performance, it's important to focus on enjoying the process of competing.

When you wake up on the morning of a game or big performance, say, "Hello Morning! Thank you! I get to compete today!" Because both the day and being an athlete are a gift. You *get to compete*. And what's also true is competition is an opportunity. You think it's a "test" because you're being timed or judged, there's a score, people are watching, and a game is on the line. But, it's how you look at it.

If you want to feel nervous, think "test." If you want to feel optimistic, think "opportunity!" It's a chance to show your skills after hours, weeks, and months of training. And it's a chance to get real gritty and gutsy, show your opponent you can kick their butt! Ha! You also get to perform with teammates if you're on a team, and support and cheer for each other. It's a day to celebrate everyone together in your sports community.

GOOD LUCK TO YOU!
LIVE YOUR DREAM!!
HIT PAY DIRT!!!

Now, if you're injured, or for some reason can't give 100% effort, that's fine. Create a different strategy and goal; it's a "progress game." Take things one step at a time.

And notice, competition requires people to be there for you in sports. You cannot compete alone, by yourself. You need opponents, coaches, officials, and usually an audience. This is community. So get in tune with your positive good energy, the optimistic, "I can do anything" energy. Smile big. Shake a hand and say, "Good Luck!"

Need Your Opponent, then Kick their Butt

My mom and I used to pray before my practices and *always* before competition. When I was eleven and preparing for a meet, we were in the car, I was in my leotard and sweats. Our eyes were closed, we were holding hands, and my mom began: "Let Lisa do her best, make her tricks, and stick her dismounts, and…" my mom added, "and may *all* the girls do their *best*, today."

I looked over at her, thinking: *Really? Everyone do their best? Not just me?* We both ended the prayer, "Amen…" and we walked into the meet.

That sounded odd, but what followed was my education, specifically in sports, to wish everyone well. We wished that all my opponents would have a positive attitude, be safe, and perform their best. It definitely sounded weird at first. I was very competitive as a gymnast, and though good luck is a nice thing to say to your opponent, my mom's intention was truly different. She really believed that winning wasn't the most important, but that competition helped athletes build character, take charge of their skills after much training, rise to a challenge, and do it together with a competitive spirit. Competition is learning and becoming your best self. So everyone, including me, will benefit by sending each other true best wishes.

I was a little confused in the beginning. I mean, why focus any real attention on an opponent? Why send anyone else good energy?

My mom demonstrated to me with her actions and words: 'Bless' your opponents and you will enjoy competition…even master it. As I watched my mom, I developed an increasing openness and positive spirit. My mom warmly greeted girls at gymnastics meets, "Good luck!" she'd smile. She sparkled as she commented on how cute their hair ribbons and ponytails were. She buzzed around other moms and said nice things like, "Isn't this exciting!" with a big grin on her face. It was amazing to watch her. She exuded an abundance of happiness as she looked into their eyes. My mom was absolutely tickled that all of the competitors were there together. It didn't matter what team they were on. She delighted in the energy and anticipation of the event: the athletes parading out on the floor, standing in straight lines, heads held high, singing the National Anthem, and marching to their first event. The competition was pure excitement for all to watch!

My mom's attitude rubbed off on me. How could it not? She was flippin' happy, and I was typically anxious to make my tricks, but I wanted to have fun, too. We bought hair clips for my teammates as good luck gifts; I wrote cards to them, and I made friends with opponents I saw regularly. Of course, I still worked my butt off in practice. I seriously focused on my back-handspring on beam, my free-hip on bars, and my Arabian-to-full on floor, because I wanted to win. But competition became more like a party than a "do or die" or "win/loss" situation. Of course, I went through nervousness. I got the most terrible butterflies. But that was because it was important to me. Then, when we got to the meet and I started to warm up, or after I raised my hand to the judge, the butterflies would go away. It grew in my mind that the meet was an opportunity to have fun, to represent my team, to perform for the judges and parents, and to compete against other gymnasts. I felt so alive at meets, doing my routines that I'd practiced over and over. I wanted to be great! And I wanted to do it while having a fabulous time. And you need your opponents to do that.

So here's the deal: You need many people in your sports community. And, even if your opponent is a jerk, or, pardon my French, a butthead, this well-wishing is worth doing. Really. Try it. Picture a tough rival in your mind. Give thanks for this opponent. Better still, wish them well! In your mind, smile, nod your head, shake hands, because you need them. And think about this: Their fiery play can only give you the best challenge for your preparation, skills, and attitude. Choose the high road to be your finest self. Your most magnificent self. Because here is the truth: When you genuinely wish someone good luck, your energy will vibrate on a higher frequency than usual because of your positive thoughts. That energy will make all doors open for you in terms of performance, and perhaps, for miracles to happen.

You need your opponent—neeeeeed. Or maybe better words are to 'respect' and 'value.' Because, without your opponent, there's no one to challenge or play against. In addition, there would be no games, and no you as an athlete. It's clear, you, by yourself, does not a sport make.

Simply put, sport is people. Sport is a powerful connection with others. And sport is life-giving. If you genuinely wish opponents the best, in a flash, you can focus back on you, your breathing, and your performance. You can bring out your own "inner tiger" to charge and attack!

The coolest part is that well-wishing is pure and good and inspiring to others. It is sport at its most magical high point. It's you, me, everyone doing something amazing—like human beings, flying. So say, "Good luck." Wish your opponent well and mean it. *Then, go kick their butt.*

How do I play my best? Create Mental Goals and Focus on your Inner Game

Your body has been trained. It's ready. Yet, athletes are consumed with being great, "I have to hit this shot," or "I have to make this pass," and that's where you get caught—stuck. You want the result. But in order to play your best, your thoughts need focus. What thoughts do you want to have during your competition? Here is a short list that may work for you:

1. Be ready for anything, because anything can happen

2. Stay calm and take a breath when things get tough

3. Keep positive and let go of mistakes and the score, move forward

4. Bring humor with me

5. Visualize, see and feel my moves, before my turn or next play

6. Remember, I only control myself

Strategies and Logistics the Week of Competition

When you feel completely ready for a game or match, you will be more emotionally at ease. Confidence will rise inside you. To mentally prepare, gather all the competition information, plan your food, sleep, uniform, and visualize! Communicate with your coach to confirm location and times, talk to team-mates about any details and the fun you're going to have. Keep it positive!

1. Seven days before your next competition: Get the location of the meet or game—name of school, gym, pool or field, and city and address and post it on your refrigerator, in your room, or in your e-Calendar.

Eat healthy foods, take vitamins, plenty of water all week.

Good sleep each night (8 hours at least); sleep is vital in order to have energy and recover from practices and a sore body. Plan which uniform you'll wear, including socks or any accessory, and make sure it's clean two days beforehand. Don't totally rely on your parents. Visualize the place you will compete—if you've been there before. Each night, imagine yourself in the meet, game, or race, doing well. Do this with breathing and relaxing, at night, for 5 minutes or more.

2. Two days before your competition: Plan your ride: who will drive or how you will get to the game location. Find out. And always arrive 15 minutes earlier than you're told, if possible, so consider your leaving time.

Get enough sleep. The two nights before your competition are the most important. It's hard to play "catch up" if you've been lacking sleep. Your body will not be fresh and strong on game day.

Plan your food for the night before, and the day of your competition. Check with your parents, the kitchen where you live, or which restaurants are nearby to make sure you'll have the foods you want to eat. Before bedtime, visualize how you will feel, what thoughts you want to have, and how you will perform in your competition.

3. The day of your competition: Plan your food and what time you'll eat that day. If you're traveling, make sure you know which restaurant and when they're open. ## If you compete or play in the morning, know that it takes 2-3 hours for your muscles to be fully "awake" and ready to perform. Plus, you need to eat a pre-game meal and digest it, prior to physical competition. If you start playing at 8 a.m., then get out of bed no later than 6 a.m.. If you play at 10 a.m., I suggest you get up at 7:00 or 7:30 a.m.. If you don't play till night time, like 7:00 p.m., then take a short rest in the middle of the day, maybe 1:00 or 2:00 p.m., if possible. Just lie down for 20 minutes, visualize, listen to soft music, keep it mellow. Then get up and take a walk, stretch, or do any mild activity for 20-30 minutes. Throughout an entire day, your body cycles through 'waves' of energy: low, medium, and high—then cycles again. So don't sit on the couch all day, or do homework all day. Mix it up. Get up, move, clean or cook, then rest a little. Then prepare for your game. Put on your uniform, bring extra supplies of anything you might need—tape, extra socks, hair bands, good luck charm. Pack a snack and water for your game. Visualize before the match; again, click into your confident mind, your muscle memory; think about how you want to feel and perform. Can you think of anything else? Okay! Say, "I've worked hard. I'm prepared and I'm ready!"

The Card

They said it was a "Re-building Year." You know, no expectations…just do your best…we're not a powerful, big team… Ha.

"They" didn't know.

Utah Gymnastics didn't rest under Greg Marsden. Our coach was tougher, wiser, and meaner than a hungry lion. The team had lost several seniors to graduation, and a junior and sophomore to early retirement; we were young and small in numbers. There were only eight of us, where most teams had ten to twelve. But so what!? In the fall of 1982, Utah was the current National Champion. In fact, 2-time National Champs, back-to-back wins in '81 and '82, and Greg *intended* to keep on winning.

I entered the University of Utah as a scholarship freshman in the fall of '82—and found myself in a pressure cooker. We lived by the clock, practices were tight, and everyone was serious. Even the air called out, "Work, work, work!" The team was led by the only two juniors, Megan McCunniff and Linda Kardos. We had no seniors. And these ladies got down to business. Serious business. At the end of two weeks of double practices, Marsman (Greg) had murdered us. With tons of basics, drills, and conditioning, we were in terrible pain. We couldn't move. Legally, we were half-dead. Then Linda and Megan huddled us together. No coaches, just the girls.

There were eight of us sweaty gymnasts standing in a circle, and the sophomores and juniors eyed me and the other freshman, Cheryl. They stood in front of us with a glare. Linda pointed at us: "We want to tell you something. We've won Nationals the last two years, and we're going to win *every year* we're on this team. So you're either with us or you're not!"

She didn't flinch. No one did. It was scary.

But I liked it… Because I wanted to win, too!

That whole year I was trying to live up to what others expected. And I learned about *real pain.* At the end of four-hour practices, Greg took us to the tunnel for sprints: an uphill, stone grey tunnel that was empty and dim.

He stood at the top and gave orders: "You're running 20 sprints. If you're slow, we'll add more. If you need to throw up, here's a bucket." He dropped one down by his feet. "Let's go!"

I can't tell you all the huffing and puffing, the wincing and moaning, the loud footsteps echoing, and the quiet tears streaming down faces...how much it hurt... And Greg barked "Go! Go! Go!" And yes, there was vomiting. (Thank god, not me.) But we paid the price right there in that dark tunnel...

We also worked with Dr. Keith Henschen; we called him "Hench." Our wise and funny sport psychologist. He taught us how to understand Greg's personality, how to disconnect from the sporadic fury, and best of all, how to get calm inside. He took us through guided meditation, breathing and relaxing, how to visualize our skills and hitting in competition. Hench told us to connect to our inner power and imagine our own success. With all of the challenges we faced, Dr. Henschen helped us believe in our own power. We knew he was the glue, the voice of possibility; he mended our brains...and yeah, he was the magic.

Pre-season charged forward and we prepared. Greg talked to us in future tense, "You will be the most consistent team! You will have the best form! And we *will be* in the best shape of any team on the floor!" He was so clear and sure, we felt his confidence and his belief. And since we were doing the work...and his words echoed strength and stamina into our minds...we believed it, too.

Over three months of competition, we marched into meets, heads held high, sparked audiences, and we won almost every one. For six months, 20 hours a week, we practiced being tough. We trained to be invincible. But at NCAA Regionals, something happened. The reigning NCAA National beam and all-around champion, our own sophomore at Utah, Sue Stednitz...had an accident. She landed a beam dismount and her knee went sideways. Sue tore her ACL—and she was out. We barely qualified for Nationals.

Now there were only seven gymnasts.

Two weeks later, NCAA Nationals was going to be held at the University of Utah, on our home court. No one thought we had a chance to win, because we were so small and broken. I was scheduled for knee surgery to remove a cyst and fix the lateral meniscus. Elaine was scheduled for ankle surgery, and she had been training just two weeks to compete all-around and fill in for Sue's events. And then Linda, one of our captains, limped into the training room just two hours before competition, crying that she rolled her ankle! What? *What?* We were plunging down a hole, a desperate dark hole. But we had trained for this, right? To fight all problems, overcome struggles, make it to Nationals and win. Somehow, we had to hold it together. But the local newspapers had stated the facts. We did not have a good chance. And worst of all, we were losing our inner strength…We were filled with doubt.

After warm ups, the seven of us were hanging by threads, taped up, in our sweats, prepared to enter the arena. It was filled with over ten thousand people, CBS TV cameras, and sports commentators. An excited "buzz" floated out of the arena and into the hallway, our hallway at the bottom of the north tunnel. And there, lined up, were the 12 best Division I college teams in the country. The best college athletes in the United States. We waited, ready to march out to compete.

Someone suddenly came up to us and said, "Utah? I have a card for you."

This was odd. We were moments from marching out. Megan took the card and we gathered 'round. A white envelope said "Utah." She opened it and pulled out the card. We had no idea who it was from… The cover said "CONGRATULATIONS!!!!" with shiny sparkles all over it.

We were confused… Then Megan opened it. And the card said,

We screamed. We laughed and screamed so loud, we jumped up and down and hugged each other. I swear, the card was a crystal ball from our magical Henschen. He said we already won. And for some crazy reason, we believed it.

We marched out into the arena and the roar of 10,000 people stood up clapping and cheering for Utah, and we…we had a party. You couldn't wipe the grins off our faces. We just had fun. And like every skill and routine we had visualized in our minds a thousand times, we hit, hit, hit every routine on the competition floor.

We were the 1983 NCAA National Champions. Three consecutive wins. Plus, Megan won the All-Around title, Linda was second in the country on beam, Elaine was the Vault Champion, and me, a freshman, I placed as the 4th best All-Around college gymnast in the country.

People wonder, how did we do it? Well, it was not an accident. We trained very hard and planned our success in our minds for months. But the other reason, our incredible opponents, missed, they tightened up and fell under pressure. Meanwhile, we felt joy. We had it in our minds what we could do, and we saw it. And I believe that we simply *believed*. Because to us, it wasn't competition. It was who we were on the floor. Like Henschen's card said, we were champions.

What if?

What if my ankle starts hurting? What if I fall? What if I mess up? What if I lose? What if I get embarrassed? What if…? Yeah, these won't help you. All negative thoughts. But you can play the "What-if game" in a fun positive way that *can help*:

Change negative 'what if' messages to

What if I hit?
What if I make great plays?
What if I/we win?
What if they give me a key to the city and throw a parade in my honor?

Haha, how fun is that! Silly, but you get the point. Imagine excellent results. Then let go. Focus on your game, get in tune with being calm and focused. And realize you create your reality. If you let your mind wander into negative "what-ifs," then you may just manifest what you're worried about. So keep a positive mind! Go out there and make your dream come true.

"New Day"

Break down your competition into parts. Each part is a New Day! The sun comes up and you start again. New time to feel re-energized, re-focused, re-connected with your inner power. For a golfer, the 'back-nine,' or every hole is a new day. For a basketball player, each quarter is a new day. For a gymnast, each event is new. For all athletes, each time you pause and re-start, come off the bench, go into another heat or race, begin a new half, every portion of play can be thought of as a "New Day." Imagine, you woke up, sun is up, and you have a fresh start. The past is the past. Get into the present moment, because you get a new chance to play your best.

★ Kick-butt Practices and Exercises for Chapter 9 ★

Exercise: Preparation & Strategy 2 Days Before

Here's a checklist for you to be mentally prepared for your next game or competition…

1. Plan your ride, who will drive or how you will get to the game location?
2. Plan to arrive 15 minutes earlier than warm-ups, if possible.
3. Get 8 hours of sleep each night.
4. Make sure your uniform is clean and you have accessories packed.
5. Plan your food for the night before, and the day of your competition. Check with nearby restaurants when traveling.
6. Before bedtime, close your eyes and peacefully visualize the competition— how you will feel, what thoughts you want to have, and how you will perform.

Exercise: Focus on Mental Goals for your Competition, Win Mentally

Think about positive thoughts and encouragement you want to give yourself on "Game Day." What mental phrases help you focus? What words make you feel powerful, calm, accurate…? This is not "I will kick straight," or "I will make 3 shots." That is physical. This is "I will *focus* on my foot moving straight," or "I will *let go* of the score" and "stay *in tune* with myself." Write down 3-5 mental goals for yourself— what you will focus on to win mentally. Here are two ideas, below, to get you going.

1. Be ready for anything, and choose a positive response.
2. Stay calm and take a breath when things get tough.

Exercise: Wish Everyone Well

If you know your opponent, before your match, plan on shaking hands, or smiling and saying, "Good luck." Go up to anyone you can, coaches, officials, and say, "Hi!" or "Good morning!" The more positive words and energy you put out—for a few minutes—toward others, that will return to you a hundred fold. Then focus on your own preparation.

Exercise: Get in Your Bubble

At the competition or game, take a few minutes to be with yourself, to be quiet, and connect to your inner voice and power. Breathe…relax your muscles…and get inside your own world, your own mental bubble. Then you can use that focus for playing, whether you are an individual athlete, or on a team.

Exercise: Detach and Play

Sometimes, athletes take games too seriously. You are too attached to having your best game, or having to win. It's freaking you out. So…detach. Let go of the result! You've done the physical training, you've mentally prepared, now relax.

One idea is to *play a fun game*. At a meet at Cal-State Fullerton, while I was competing for Utah, we sat on the floor in a circle instead of immediately warming up. We played the game "Telephone." We whispered into each other's ear a message and passed it around the circle to see how the last person goofed it up. Ohh, we laughed so hard. After 15 minutes, we warmed up looser, quicker, and felt more confident. That loose, fun approach intimidated our opponent. They were so confused. Meanwhile, we had fun and ended up winning! Play a game if you can, even a solo game. Or bring a funny picture or a stuffed animal. But—lighten up!

Chapter 10
Body Smart: The Wise will Excel

Sport is Body in Motion

Being in tune with your body, caring for it, and appreciating it, is vital for an athlete. Regarding mental skills, you will practice awareness of your body's design, what it can do, and the fact you can nurture it and assist the healing process with injuries. Being in charge of your knowledge, thoughts, and physical body means you are cultivating a stronger approach to training. In this chapter, you can enhance your body-knowledge.

Your body-knowledge directly effects your self-perception, emotions, how you prepare for competition, and how well you perform. This short chapter is not intended to teach you everything. No. Sports doctors, trainers, physical therapists, sport psychologists, and nutritionists are the professionals. I am a connector, and as a mental skills coach, I'm simply touching on the importance of the psychological aspect in sports, of being in tune with your body. I invite you to look at resources in a library, bookstore, or online so you can learn more. Be curious and go for it!

Best Athletes Understand and Care for Their Bodies

DNA: the molecular make-up you get from your biological parents

Body type: shapes or categories of the human physique

Sports Nutrition: how to fuel your body properly for performance

Rest, Treatment, Recovery: how to manage preventative care and injury care

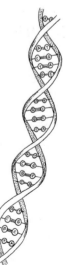

DNA: Your Genetic Design

The first fact is your DNA came from your biological parents. If you're not pleased with your body or how you look, consider this perspective: Your DNA is absolutely unique; you are the only person in the world like you, so own that fact. Be proud to be you. And you will inherit a combination of features from each of your birth parents. If one of them is short, maybe you'll be short. If they're muscular, you'll be muscular. Also, if they have dark skin or light skin, bingo, you, too, or a nice blend of color. If you're father has a hairy chest, then, a hairy chest you could get (well…probably just the guys). The point is, your physical make-up comes from your biological parents through DNA. You were predetermined, destined, so learn to work with it.

Whether a boy or girl, man or woman, we often criticize our bodies instead of *embracing* what we have. We want to look like someone else, someone taller, more muscular or leaner, with toned legs or a tiny waist… But, the truth is you are perfectly made. And you are a miracle. Including your pinky toes. And if you're jealous of others, if you sit in misery and self-criticism, that only leads to negative thoughts and negative energy. **If you don't cherish your thighs, then love your belly button, nose, or cute ears! Because, negative thoughts about your body hurt your performance.** Read again—negative thoughts *hurt* your performance. Surround yourself with people who are smart, kind, and appreciate your individuality, who compliment and say positive words to you. Because you are unique. You are the only you, and when you enjoy that, you will more likely be a positive, vibrant athlete.

Body Type: Shapes and Categories

Three general body types are slim, round, and muscular. But we are all a mixture of those, no one is 100% muscular, or 100% curvy, or any other. And there's also height: tall, average, short. All humans are a combination of these.

For athletes, it's helpful to know *traditional* body types for certain sports. But brace yourself, many of us are *not* traditional, so get comfortable with it.

- For a slim, linear body, you could be a marathon runner or tennis player
- For a round, curvy body, perhaps a power-lifter or rugby player
- For the muscular, triangular body type, you might be a rower or a gymnast

As I noted, some of us break the body-sport tradition. I am nearly 5'8" and *very tall* for a gymnast. I am King Kong. Average *Elite* gymnasts stand a mere 5'0" tall, and I towered over them. This was not easy for me, I will be honest. In terms of body image and self-esteem, I felt so big that I struggled for a while and did not care for myself. I was depressed. I felt panicky, restless, and not confident at all. I was consumed with my body. After a couple months, I decided, finally, to let go of that obsession, because it was destroying my happiness. And I was not doing great in the gym, either. I realized the key is to feel balanced in all aspects of sport and life. I needed to find peace in my mind and be a great athlete and person the way I was made. I got support and talked with someone. And if you're ever in trouble, talk to someone, a coach, parent, or especially a doctor. They will help you. But there is evidence of untraditional bodies all around us in other sports and these athletes do great things. For example, some college and professional basketball players are as short as 5'9" and do extremely well. So don't be discouraged if you're different, and please care for your lovely body. It's what you were given and it can do amazing things.

Check out the fabulous photo exhibit and the variety of body shapes in the book "Athlete" by Howard Schatz. There are photographs of 125 champion athletes, which truly show that we are all beautiful and unique.

Embrace your body type!

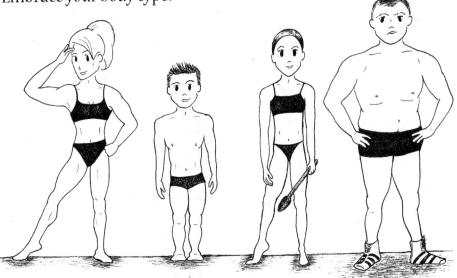

Sports Nutrition: Fuel your body to train, perform, and heal

Is your sport mainly endurance or power? Aerobic or anaerobic? Each sport requires a certain energy output. For example, a food plan for a ballet dancer will be different from a football player. Food and energy for a sprinter contrasts with the needs of a long distance swimmer. With a parent, coach, trainer, or doctor, learn your needs. Learn how to train and fuel your fabulous body for peak performance; read materials about your physical needs in relation to your sport. Teach yourself to choose healthy foods and vitamin supplements to increase your energy, heal injuries, and recover quickly. Learn your strengths and weaknesses. How can you improve your fitness and best prepare your body? With proper fuel (food), you can make improvements to increase your body's abilities. When you eat and train a certain way, you can get stronger, faster, more agile, and more accurate. Plus, food is brain fuel as well.

Your mind will feel sharper, more focused, and more confident when you eat healthy! Food is medicine!

I recommend meeting with a sports nutritionist, if you truly want to learn the best and current information. I highly recommend *Nancy Clark's Sports Nutrition Guide Book*. Look her up online: Nancy Clark, sports nutritionist. She's thorough and completely awesome! And her materials are very friendly, smart, and cover all types of athletes' needs. She recommends nutrient-dense foods, homemade smoothies, vitamins, easy grab-and-go snacks, and even has recipes...I love her.

And afterwards, after you burned many calories and expended all your energy, food and nutrients help your body to heal, recover, and re-energize...

Rest, Treatment, Recovery

Sleep: Athletes often underestimate how important it is to allow your body to rest and recover. To perform your best, the body needs to feel fresh and alive! Prepare for practices and games by getting good sleep. Heal injuries and do better in school with plenty of sleep. After hard practices, competitions, or games, you will recover best with rest. Especially if you have back-to-back practices or multi-day games, 7-8 hours of sleep is imperative (maybe more, depending on your age and body's needs). Make sure you learn what is best for you. Check out the National Sleep Foundation, or Fatigue Science; look up sleep for athletes. This is very important for you to be informed, fully rested, and ready to go after it!

Hydrate: Drink lots of water, please. This is another area that athletes rarely read about—replacing lost fluids to hydrate and replenish electrolytes. As you sweat, you lose fluids. It's super important to drink, drink, drink water and

electrolyte drinks (like Gatorade), or make sure you have proper sodium intake. Do you know how much is enough for your body, your weight, and your sport? For endurance athletes, you don't want to cramp up, and it's important for all athletes to hydrate. Find out. Ask your coach, parent, or a nutritionist, or look it up! See Nancy Clark Sports Nutrition, she's great! Or Active.com. There's ample information online. Have fun!

Treat Injuries: If you have aches and pains, or a nagging, recurring injury, find out from a medical professional what is best. Athletes benefit from having a good sports doctor and athletic trainer. But initially, if a hand or foot is sore or swollen yet you can still practice, then do 'training room' treatments at home to help. I am not a medical professional, so you need to check in with your parents and follow a doctor or trainer's recommendation.

You can learn simple home practices for swollen or sore muscles and joints, like, R.I.C.E. Rest, Ice, Compression, Elevation. Many athletes do this at home, or even on the road at a hotel for away-games. I will give a brief description, but check with a doctor or trainer to make sure you are taking proper steps. RICE starts with *Resting* the injury. Get off your feet. Lie down or prop your limb on a pillow while reading. *Elevate* the body part (ankle, knee, wrist…) up higher than your heart, if possible. *Ice* the hurt area for 15-20 minutes at a time, two or three rounds of icing in a sitting. *Compression* is wrapping the swollen area, and don't wrap too tightly! Just apply some pressure. Another note, you can also do self-massage, light pressure, and circular motions with your fingers, to keep blood flowing. If you have inflammation/swelling, it may be recommended to take Motrin or Ibuprofen, an over-the-counter anti-inflammatory. Again, the key is *take care of your body.* Check with your medical professional to learn what's best. Read online for good articles. And feel good about taking charge of your body for sports. You are an intelligent athlete.

Stay curious! Keep learning, and you will keep advancing in sport and life.

Chapter 11
Divine Grace in Sport

Your Human Spirit

As an athlete, you do many workouts, sweat buckets, and plan to do your best, but then on *the day of competition*, there are many things out of your control. Even though you've trained and set a plan, anything can happen. So after you prepare, there's that element of "luck" or "chance" or…whatever the universe brings. And I believe the universe returns what you put out. You know, the law of attraction.

I also believe in our human spirit, and something 'bigger' than me. Amazing things happen in sports and life when you believe in something bigger than you, or something very important, more important than winning. For instance, in the Olympic Games, it's common to see extraordinary performances. Athletes describe in interviews how they feel so grateful to compete, they are privileged to represent their country, and they want to honor their home and people; those feelings inspire them to be extraordinary!

Another example, have you ever seen a team at a game, and on every player's uniform they're wearing a special patch or band on their sleeve? That patch is dedicated to someone who is ill or just passed away. The team is honoring that person by wearing the patch and playing their best. They're sending out a loving spirit. Plus, they want to let everyone know. This type of enthusiasm also catches the audience's attention, and collectively, that "love" produces a vibrant force within a team, a fantastic energy. The team plays with more strength and vitality; they are more focused and psyched up, and often, that team wins the game. Because when you believe in something more important or bigger than yourself, you let go of your ego to win, and the fear of losing. You simply *rise*, because you're driven by your spirit. Your human spirit. And amazing things happen.

What is Divine Grace in Sport?

Divine means heavenly or celestial.

Grace means favor or goodwill.

Divine Grace: a favor from heaven.

Believing in the 'idea' of a heavenly favor is not always easy. Most people want proof in advance that a favor will come. But what is true in the mind, is when you relax, you allow newness to come in. When you surrender the "have-to" mindset, like "I have to make this," then you are not tensing or forcing. You are in a different attitude, trusting your talent and training, and that good things will happen. You connect to your human spirit in a way that is extraordinary. Consider Olympic athletes who have gone through injuries and hardships only to compete in the Olympic Games to represent their country and to trust. They trust goodness will come; and in that Olympic spirit, they break world records and do things we didn't *think* was possible. They even surprise themselves.

Some people think we learn about grace and God only through religion and church. But for me, it was in sports that I *first experienced* what we may call… Divine Grace.

You Can't Fall!

I was training and competing a side aerial on beam. If you don't know, that's a cartwheel with no hands, on a 4-inch beam, four feet in the air. I was 12 years old and I was struggling to stay on the beam.

Several days before a competition, I told my mom in the car, "I think I'm going to take out my side aerial and not compete it. It's not consistent, I keep falling." It was only the two of us in the car.

She turned and looked at me with her curly smile and happy eyes, "Lisa, there's nothing to worry about…"

What? How could she say that? I wanted to hit my beam routine in the meet.

She went on, "Don't you know…? You can't fall!" I didn't understand, and she continued, "You can't fall, God is holding you up!"

Now I'd heard everything. She's nuts.

"Lisa," she continued, "God is like the marionette and you're the puppet. He's up there and you're on the beam. The strings go from God, up there (she looked up to heaven), down to you on the beam…he's got you, he's holding you up. *You can't fall!*"

I rolled my eyes and grinned at the ridiculous idea… But I couldn't help imagine a white bearded man in a white robe, in the clouds, holding me up with strings while I stood on the beam. It was so weird, as if God can keep me on the beam. My mom was glowing, she even giggled. I thought, *She's off her rocker*, but she repeated it, "You can't fall!"

It was really silly, but my mom's crazy suggestions were often good ones, so I thought about it…

A few days later, I was warming up at the competition on beam. I was trying hard. I attempted the side aerial three times and didn't make one. Frustration hit me. *I'm still falling!* That made me tighten up more. Warms-ups concluded and I had to sit and wait for my turn to compete. Wait, wait, wait… I sat there with no confidence. None. I began to ponder the crazy: the whole God-marionette, me-puppet idea. When it was my turn, I took a big breath, sighed, and decided: *Fine…! I surrender. God will hold me up.*

Again, weird. But…when I surrendered, I let go of having to hit my routine. And almost instantly, the tension I had been feeling drifted away. I raised my hand to the judge and mounted the beam, and my brain went quiet. I moved along easily like I was folding laundry. My mind was loose, my body flowed, and I came to the side aerial… I didn't "try," I just threw my body into the air and the wildest thing—I made it! My feet landed on the beam and I stuck it! I finished my routine like clockwork, easily. My coach and teammates wondered how I appeared so relaxed. I couldn't explain it. I knew I let go of my tension, but hitting the side aerial right in front of the judges, that felt like a gift from heaven. And I call it *divine grace*.

Let Your Body Do

I learned that when I surrendered, I relaxed. I let my body do its thing. When I was trying super hard, I clenched and tightened; I was fighting myself. When I let go, I trusted my body and it flowed. Honestly, it doesn't matter who triggers the trust—for me it was my mom suggesting it, and using the image of God holding me up. But ultimately, I stopped thinking and trying and just trusted my body would know what to do. Not needing to force a skill, not controlling or trying too hard, I let go of all my tension and worry. In the flow, you perform at a higher level. And at that moment…anything is possible!

Sport is Togetherness, Sport is Spirit

In sport, you are not alone. All participants, coaches, parents, officials, all of us are together. And by virtue of being together, cheering for each other, we experience a collective energy. As humans, *we feel*…we are emotional creatures, feeling creatures. Without words, without touch, we have enormous impact on each other because of the energy we exude. And without words, your energy goes out into the world. Whenever you are inspired, you are in-spirit. You are a spiritual being, and that is powerful and amazing.

With that spirit, you overcome difficult moments and can imagine and do great things! You experience a natural high. Have you felt it? It's a rush! And in that mindset—and vast ocean of possibility—you trust and take risks. You take risks to catch a ball, stop or hit a ball, or fly through the air on skis or ice skates, or over a beam or a hurdle. You *believe* in real and good possibilities when you fire-up your body in sports. You *believe* you will catch a ball, make a goal, hit a home run, make a shot, and land on your feet. Something good will happen! People around you send good energy to you. And when you or your team are behind, struggling, yet you trust, *your mind and heart trusts you will rise*, an incredible performance comes through divine grace.

I don't talk about God much, but I have a strong faith. Growing up, my mom and dad described God as a loving God, a happy dancing God, a God that celebrates our efforts and is always with us. I began to let my mind tune into "a presence," a positive force in and around me, and the positive energy of others. It felt like this invisible 'love' supported and lifted me up whenever I needed it. And I struggled a lot, so I needed it a lot.

I think about that, and a positive presence is with me every day. All I have to do is pause and remember my human spirit. My spirit connects with people everywhere, and I believe in all the good possibilities in life. Even during a struggle, I hope you believe that your best intentions and inspired thoughts create wonderful moments in sports. I hope you imagine something over and over, and you work real hard for it, and believe you can achieve it. Right now, I can imagine your eyes dancing, your heart beating, and your desire growing as you read these words. I believe you can master your mind and achieve your goals. The question is…*do you?*

People and Resources are Everywhere

Because of the internet, all around the world we are connected. And you can find all the info you desire. I recommend the following sites, people, and organizations, but it's really just a start. It's a spark to get your fire going! Enjoy the journey of exploration and advancing your knowledge and reaching goals in sports and in life.

Quiet Places

Meditation centers offer wonderful classes in learning awareness and how to manage thoughts; they also offer quiet sitting, guided meditation, and insightful talks for young people. There are centers in many cities and towns. Look for one near you and check it out!

I often go to IMC in Redwood City, CA:

http://www.insightmeditationcenter.org/

Dr. Amy Saltzman is a friend of mine and she is a pioneer in Mindfulness and educating kids, parents, coaches, and athletes in the practice of managing thoughts and emotions and how to connect to the still quiet place inside you. Perhaps you will like her website and what she offers:

http://www.stillquietplace.com/

Inner balance and wellness helps athletes to gain more ease and accuracy in sports. Deepak Chopra has incredible programs and information that may stir your mind and guide you in a healthy direction:

www.chopra.com

Sport Psychology

These books are profound and important They are my "bibles;" I use them all the time! They cover the full variety of issues in sport psychology and team dynamics, including the coach's point of view, as well as athletes' experiences. If you are interested in studying sport psychology, the Routledge Handbook is ideal. Note: I co-authored Chapter 5!

The Inner Game of Tennis: The Classic Guide to the Mental Side of Peak Performance, by W. Timothy Gallwey.

In Pursuit of Excellence, by Terry Orlick.

Routledge Handbook of Applied Sport Psychology: A Comprehensive Guide for Students and Practitioners, by Stephanie J. Hanrahan, Mark B. Andersen.

Sacred Hoops: Spiritual Lessons of a Hardwood Warrior, by Phil Jackson and Hugh Delehanty.

To find out more about your mind and resources for athletes, parents, coaches, and more on fitness, health, injury, and rehabilitation, look here:

http://www.appliedsportpsych.org/

The Positive Coaching Alliance (PCA) is a fantastic organization that promotes and educate healthy ways to seek achievement in sports, whether that's improvement, or a big win. They have all kinds of books and resources, and they even have Youth Awards.

http://www.positivecoach.org/

Dr. Ken Ravizza trained me in sport psychology, and I learned and applied the tools; I had lots of success with the mental skills. He has been ground-breaking in his methods, working with athletes and teams and teaching them insight.

http://www.peaksports.com/sports-psychology-blog/mental-coaching-with-dr-ken-ravizza/

Dr. Keith Henschen was our team sport psychologist in college at the University of Utah. He is simply amazing. He's worked with Olympians and professional athletes, and I am grateful he coached me!

http://www.peaksports.com/sports-psychology-blog/whole-athlete-training-with-dr-keith-henschen/

Sports Organizations and Competitions

The Olympic movement is a global effort to bring athletes and countries together in the spirit of human performance. How exciting to be motivated and inspired by the Olympics. Look at these websites and spark yourself and your dreams.

https://www.olympic.org/youth-olympic-games

https://www.olympic.org/

When you are college bound or competing in college, you can always check in with the NCAA and their resources to help athletes, coaches, and teams.

http://www.ncaa.org/

NCAA Eligibility Center is an important step to make sure athletes are eligible for the college recruiting process, and eligible to play sports in college.

http://www.ncaa.org/student-athletes/future/how-register

Healthy Body, Good Food, Plenty of Sleep

American Physical Therapy Association has a site called "Move Forward" which has great tips for athletes when dealing with injuries, rehab, and taking care of your body.

http://www.moveforwardpt.com/SymptomsConditions.aspx

Nancy Clark is one of my favorites when it comes to Sports Nutrition! Her books and information are very informative, helpful, and friendly. She has tips for every athlete in every sport. Check her out!

http://www.nancyclarkrd.com/

Body Image issues can impact an athlete's view of themselves and hinder how they approach training and competing. A positive view of your body, feeling strong and fit, is key.

https://sports.good.is/features/female-athlete-body-image

http://mymodernmet.com/howard-schatz-beverly-ornstein-athlete/

http://www.ncaa.org/health-and-safety/sport-science-institute/whole-image-athletes-body-image-enhancement-disordered-eating-prevention-online-program

Sleep is a priority for performing well in sports. There is a lot of information out there.

https://www.fatiguescience.com/blog/5-ways-sleep-impacts-peak-athletic-performance/

https://sleepfoundation.org/

Work hard, sleep well, and dream big!

Acknowledgments

It took many people throughout my life to nurture, educate, and bring me to this place to be able to create this book. I could never have done it without the proper teachers, role models, and necessary loved ones. From the very beginning my parents, Jim and Lorie Mitzel, have been a fountain of love and support. They were brave to have seven children, and in our family they modeled what it was to sacrifice, persist, and be dedicated to activities with purpose. They never doubted what was possible, and I continue to experience their amazing joy of life and the wisdom to guide me through it. Thank you, Mom and Dad, forever. My siblings, Sheila, Jimmy, Patrick, Julie, Mikey and Brian, you're totally awesome. You played with me, helped me to use my imagination, taught me to be thoughtful and share, and you certainly shaped my competitive spirit! I am so grateful for all of you, your families, and your love. To my children, Weston, McKenna, and Conrad, thank you for being so patient and supportive when I was in graduate school and every time I sat to read or write at the computer. You are so bright, smart, and fun. I am the luckiest mom to have you in my life and to have practiced my teaching methods with you! haha.

To all of my club coaches at Heck's and Kips, especially Glynn Heckenlaible, Jim Fountaine, and Mary Wright. Thank you for welcoming me, challenging me, teaching me discipline and artistry, and for your endless energy in coaching. To all my teammates at Heck's Gymnastics and Kips Gymnastics; you embraced me, motivated me, and lifted me up.

For recruiting me, giving me a scholarship, and being my coach at the University of Utah, I will always feel the deepest gratitude to Greg Marsden. Through your diligence, vision, and voice, you opened up a higher potential in me that I didn't know was there. With the Utah Gymnastics staff, including Tyler McOmber, Dr. Bill Sands, Anne Marie Jensen, Chip Schaefer, Jeff Wilcox, Dr. Bill Bean, Terri Warner, Donna Cozzo, Sam Varner, and Steve Varechok, you helped make me a stronger person, more aware of myself and others, and taught me how to become a champion on the inside. And Liz Abel, your devotion to the program has been done with the utmost integrity and fire, and your friendship has been paramount to me. To my Utah teammates, Megan McCunniff-Marsden, Linda Kardos, Elaine Alfano, Celeste Harrington, Cindy Paul, Sue Stednitz, Cheryl Milgrom, Tina Hermann, Sandy Sobotka, Lynn Lederer, Cheryl Weatherstone, Kim Taylor, Caralee Novak, Lisa McVay, Wendy Whiting, Hilarie Portell, and Sonja Ahone, your honesty, tenacity, commitment, and love of competition showed me a gutsy confidence that drove my desire and made us a close family. You are forever my sisters. Your words and can-do spirit have given me a lifetime of resilience and positivity, and I feel you are with me all the time.

Dr. Ken Ravizza and Dr. Keith Henschen, what precious gifts you are in my life. As sport psychologists with humor and warmth, I was able to learn patience, trust in the process, and with your insight and guidance, the ability to overcome the hardest times in my sports career…and reach my dreams. My gratitude for all your work and all you've done for me is pouring out. And I must add the awesome coach, Lynn Rogers! Without all three of you, this book would not be possible.

To Breck Greenwood and Stanford Athletics, for hiring me and supporting me as a Women's Gymnastics coach at Stanford University. I learned so much! Thank you to the women I coached, for you trusted me and took risks, and wasn't it fun! To all the Stanford coaches past and present who have been a friend, inspired me, and championed my efforts, I am grateful.

In the Bay Area, I've been tapped with fairy dust to be able to coach at Airborne Gymnastics—thank you, Melanie Ruggiero and Leah Tanquary for your enthusiasm and trust, allowing me to coach all the competitive teams and teach mental skills. I am grateful to work with the gymnasts, use my mental training curriculum, and see the wonderful impact its had.

To my athlete-clients everywhere, especially at Airborne, Santa Ana College Track and Field, SCATS Gymnastics, NBAA, Bayshore Elite Gymnastics, and Olympus Gymnastics, you are magnificent! I've had a blast speaking with you and coaching all of you; I am honored to hear your stories and teach you mental skills. Wayne Wright and San Jose State Athletics, thanks for inviting me to speak at the Women's Summit!

To the Spalding University MFA program. You taught me more about human spirit and the skills and craft of exemplary creative writing than I imagined. Thank you, Sena Jeter Naslund, Katy Yocom, Kathleen Driskell, Karen Mann, and my excellent professors, Ellie Bryant, Luke Wallin, and Joyce McDonald.

I want to acknowledge the fantastic parents and teachers I met at PNS, Parents Nursery School in Palo Alto. You hugged my kids, let me cry, made me laugh when I needed it most, and cheered for me in my writing endeavors. Wow! For being in my life and believing in me: my second family, Rainer and Trix Dahl and all the Dahl-Crowder kids.

What would I do in my life without the best girlfriends a girl could have: Resa Winterling, Roxanne Pecadeso, Tracy Hughes, Jennifer Britton, Jennifer Anthony, Amy Saltzman, Mary Hower, Julia Zanutta, Denise Kouzoujian, and Cat Westover. Your wisdom, silliness, kindness, and support throughout the years, especially in writing this book, have been invaluable. I am a thousand-times blessed.

And to a few people who may not know their impact, but let me say that Jason Trollope, Pete Judd, and Nick Karayannis—you have touched my heart, given me courage, and sparked me to keep growing, to write, create, coach, and just be myself…thank you.

Finally, to my exquisite book designer, Judi Eichler, and astute editor, Vanessa Gonzales. You are angels, as well as incredible professionals, and exactly who I needed to work with on this project. You have kept me calm and reassured, while guiding and shaping these words and images. This book is much better because of you. My cup overflows.

Author-Illustrator

Lisa Mitzel grew up in a family of nine in Southern California. At age eight she started gymnastics, and over ten years she won State, Regional, and National titles. She also endured sprained ankles, knee surgeries, a broken back, fractured tibias and other setbacks. Pain was part of the journey. At age 15, while training for the U.S. National Team, Lisa had a terrible crash in the gym and developed traumatic psychological fears. Soon, she regressed and lost 70% of her skills and nearly quit.

Dr. Ken Ravizza, a sport psychologist, met and trained Lisa. Despite her fears she applied the mental skills, and a few months later she became a 2-Time Jr. Olympic National Champion. She went on to compete Elite and place in the top 25 in the country.

Lisa was recruited by Greg Marsden and received a full scholarship to the University of Utah. She became an NCAA 6-Time All-American, National Champion, and a member of 4 NCAA National Championship Teams. Later, Lisa was inducted into the University of Utah Hall of Fame. After college, Lisa spent time in L.A., danced professionally, and today, she continues to choreograph floor routines.

As Head Women's Gymnastics Coach at Stanford University, Lisa guided a young team to success with many All-Americans, an NCAA National top-10 finish, and started new era at Stanford. Following that, she raised three kids and earned an MFA in Writing. She wrote and produced a local sports TV show, published a chapter in Routledge Handbook of Applied Sport Psychology, and is now working on a book for parents to understand the athlete's inner world, and how to guide them to reach their goals. Finally, Lisa is a professional speaker, she also works with athletes and teams to perform with a sharp focus, a higher mind, and incredible self-belief. She lives in the Bay Area in California and is excited to keep coaching athletes, speak to groups, and share her experiences. Learn more at *LisaMitzel.com*